The
Breakaway
Cook

Also by Eric Gower

The Breakaway Japanese Kitchen

The Breakaway Cook

Recipes That Break Away from the Ordinary

Eric Gower

WILLIAM MORROW

An Imprint of HarperCollinsPublishers

HarperCollins books may be purchased for educational, business, or sales promotional use. For information please write: Special Markets Department, HarperCollins Publishers, 10 East 53rd Street, New York, NY 10022.

FIRST EDITION

Designed by Nicola Ferguson
Photographs by Annabelle Breakey

Library of Congress Cataloging-in-Publication Data

Gower, Eric.
    The breakaway cook: recipes that break away from the ordinary / Eric Gower.
        p. cm.
    ISBN: 978-0-06-085166-8
    ISBN-10: 0-06-085166-X
        1. Cookery. I. Title.

TX714.G686 2007
        641.5—dc22   2006052583

07 08 09 10 11 ❖ / TP 10 9 8 7 6 5 4 3 2 1

This book is dedicated to all of us free-wheeling
cooks who delight in new discoveries

Contents

Acknowledgments

A book project like this one reaffirms one's faith in humanity; it never ceases to amaze me how generous people can be with their time, expertise, input, and much else. Heather Drucker and Jonathan Schwartz got the ball rolling by introducing me to Harriet Bell, the grande dame of cookbook editors, who graciously and artfully guided this thing to fruition. Thanks, Harriet, for all your patience and wisdom.

My team of readers and tasters—Pat Dillon, Lucelle Hoefnagels, Dave Harp, John Wilner, Scott Ashkenaz, Julie Swan, Sarah Brayer, Sharon Fisher, Sarah Lonsdale, Steve Silberman, and Ed Ward—kept egging me on to do better, and I'm grateful to them for all their expert help. Charles Haynes and Debbie Gross yet again encouraged maximum creativity in their kitchen; it's such a pleasure to cook there. Alan and Nef Mart, partners in our joint purchases of happy, grass-fed local cows and pigs, have been culinary inspirations for more than twenty years. Two of my main breakaway boosters, Robert Carroll and Paul Braund, have played significant roles in helping me shape the form and direction of this book, and of books to come. Thanks too to Liv Blumer, my literary agent, who lent her steady and cool-headed guidance to the project from the beginning, and to website design diva Stephanie Sawchenko.

Annabelle Breakey is not only a brilliant photographer, she's one of the nicest people on the planet. Thank you, Annabelle, for your untold hours of incredibly hard work. George Dolese and Elisabet Nederlander, styling team extraordinaire, lend grace and sophistication to everything they touch (and are a total joy to be around). Jonelle Patrick trusted me with her incredible collection of Japanese ceramics, and opened up her lovely San Francisco home to the chaos of our photo shoots. Thank you, Jonelle! More thanks go to Richard Silver and Felicity O'Meara for their beautiful ceramics and props. I'm extremely grateful to Alta Tingle and the entire staff of the Gardener in Berkeley—that mecca of rustico urbanity—for lending me some of the coolest plates, bowls, and table settings I've ever seen.

And where would I be without my Lingy, the lovely and talented Delia van der Plas. Thanks for putting up with all my breakaway obsessions.

The
Breakaway
Cook

Introduction

"Breakaway" cooking is a new and powerful way for home cooks to think about what to put on the table. It's a style of cooking uniquely suited to today's dizzying array of choices of what and how to eat. It pays homage to the culinary traditions and ingredients of half a dozen or so countries, yet it breaks away from all of them to create a new and coherent way to cook.

Breakaway food is simple to prepare: it requires little or no previous cooking experience and takes little time. It's powerfully flavored and reaches far and wide for inspiration and ingredients. "Ah, fusion cooking," you might say. Not at all.

When people ask, "What's the difference between breakaway cooking and fusion?" I say that breakaway cooking is fusion that actually makes sense. Both are attracted to the combination of disparate and often surprising elements, but breakaway cooking, unlike much fusion cooking, consciously keeps things simple. Breakaway cooking is for home cooks who aren't interested in novelty for novelty's sake (in contrast to cutting-edge fusion restaurants, which constantly seek to lead the pack), but whose cooking can be improved radically with the introduction of a few key global ingredients.

I use what I call "global flavor blasts"—things like miso, pomegranate molasses, and tamarind—which are flavor-packed, intense ingredients that typically take a lot of time and care to make from scratch but are now widely, inexpensively, and conveniently available in ethnic markets and online. You can add a tremendous amount of flavor to a dish simply by incorporating some of these robust flavors into your cooking, with very little effort or expense. And a cardinal rule of breakaway cooking is to season with authority. Part of the food's vibrancy is derived from concentrated flavors that play off one another. This is especially true with salt, which forms the baseline of many of the dishes presented in this book.

Breakaway cooking is simultaneously about the fast and mindful preparation of food and about the slow savoring of that food. This is really what the "slow food" movement is about. You can, in my opinion, cook "slow food" quite quickly; it's the savoring of it that takes up so much time (usually the entire evening, if things go well). One goal of breakaway cooking is to create simple combinations of textures and tastes that make you silently pause in gratification at the interplay going on in the mouth.

Moreover, breakaway cooking stresses the power of presentation. Serve your meals on excellent pottery and use glassware and table linens that really appeal to you; all are worth splurging on, considering how much time you'll spend with them. And plating should always be simple, almost effortless—never stack or pile food in a way that requires deconstruction or even carving. As a diner, I prefer to simply lift bites into my mouth using chopsticks (wood feels much better in my mouth than metal does) and not have to do any "work" at the table at all.

Breakaway cooking also has a time/hassle component. If a dish takes two days to prepare, barely five minutes to eat, and another day to clean up properly, something's wrong. Breakaway cooking is about making great food with little to no hassle.

But breakaway cooking is about a few other things too. It's an approach to food that dissolves a lot of the tension that many of us feel about cooking and eating, about the role food plays in our lives. We all want to enjoy great food, but the never-ending battle between time constraints, creativity, and sheer information overload leaves us feeling paralyzed.

We spend so many hours of our lives shopping for food, preparing it, cooking it, consuming it, and cleaning up afterward. Most of us do it every day. If we can rise to what often feels like a tyrannical daily event without dread or fear or anxiety, it can be an anchoring presence for the other twenty-three hours of the day. Once we acknowledge and embrace the huge role that food inevitably plays in our lives, good things begin to happen.

• • •

I spent most of my twenties and thirties living in Japan, where it is very easy to walk out the door anytime and get a decent, inexpensive, and nutritious meal. Traditional, everyday Japanese cuisine is a thing of simplicity and wonder, and for years I frequented the restaurants of Kyoto and Tokyo with unflagging enthusiasm. But eventually it dawned on me that, not only did I enjoy cooking dinner at home, but I often liked the food that I cooked better too. The reason was simple: I cooked food made expressly for my own palate. I didn't care if the food I made was considered traditional or untraditional, authentic or inauthentic: the only thing I cared about was whether it tasted good. My cooking epiphany came when I realized that my palate is almighty: the only right way to cook something is to cook it so it tastes good to you. That notion is the heart and soul of breakaway cooking.

In the beginning I enjoyed the process of reproducing classic Japanese dishes, but once I mastered those, I liked tweaking dishes in ways that tasted good to me. I like eating tofu, for example, in the traditional way, with soy sauce, scallions, and grated ginger. But I also like mixing soft tofu with pomegranate molasses and egg and baking it, or drizzling it with good olive oil, fresh herbs, and sliced fruit and dusting the dish with salt and pepper. Edamame (fresh soybeans) are great just shucked and salted—pretty much the only way they're eaten in Japan—but they're even better when you puree a handful of them with a vinaigrette of choice and then dress the rest of them with that sauce. Udon is lovely in a traditional *dashi* (broth made from kelp and dried bonito), but it takes on a new life altogether when you blend mint, cilantro, fresh ginger, lemon, and olive oil and work that into the cooked noodles. Traditionalists might cry foul, but who cares? I am the one eating it.

When I moved back to San Francisco after fifteen years in Japan, I discovered that my breakaway style of cooking—using Japanese ingredients in unorthodox yet delightful ways by combining them with the best organic bounty I could find—could be expanded radically by the cornucopia of beautiful ingredients I was seeing everywhere. Indian, Middle Eastern, Chinese, and Mexican markets beckoned, and I began, much as I did in Japan, by purchasing unfamiliar ingredients and playing with them, getting to know their flavor profiles. And by combining these new (to me) tastes with whatever seasonal produce I happened to find at farmers' markets, I began to make some really good food, food that paid homage to certain ethnic culinary traditions but that broke away from the confines of "authenticity" and toward something more organic, lively, and simple. The principles of break-away Japanese cooking, I discovered, could easily be transferred to other culinary traditions.

The recipes that follow are simple to prepare. While I've tried to be clear and precise in the recipes and descriptions, I intend for them to be suggestions and guides. When you use recipes as broad outlines rather than as tight scripts (as I hope you will use mine), you tend to substitute or omit altogether some in-gredients called for in any given dish. I happen to love each one of these, yet even I, the author, seem incapable of making them the same way twice. Quite a few of the dishes were happy accidents, the result of an almost-bare fridge and a snarling stomach. The entire spirit of this book urges you to ignore anything I say in these recipes: try them as written once and then use them as a backbone or an entry point for new dishes that you'll create, given the ingredients you have on hand, time constraints, energy levels, or anything else that guides your cooking.

The metaphor is far from original, but you can use this book in the same way that a confident classical musician can sight-read any composition—by simply following what's written on the page—and thereby do the piece justice. Or you can improvise like a jazz musician and add your own flourishes and flavors and come up with different results each time. I suggest doing both. But whatever you do, take everything I say with a large grain of sea salt and use your own palate to guide you.

Salt and Pepper:
The Breakaway Workhorses

It's impossible to overstate the importance of good salt and good pepper in cooking. They are the two most important ingredients in the cuisines of most cultures, and for good reason. The proper use of salt and pepper—and by that I mean quality, not necessarily quantity—will make an average meal an exceptional one.

Salt

Arguments over salt remind me of the PC versus Mac computer imbroglios of the early days. The "salt is salt—it's all sodium chloride" crowd argues vehemently that any differences in taste are purely in the mind of the taster, that the taste buds can't tell the difference, and that the people who buy little eight-dollar canisters of French sea salt are being hoodwinked. Others say, with less ardor but equal conviction, that expensive salt actually tastes better.

My salt arsenal is vast. I use all kinds, including various sea salts and especially finishing-salt blends that I make in my spice grinder. I add interesting ingredients to sel gris (gray salt) from Brittany and then whir them together to produce unique and flavor-packed salts such as maccha salt, lavender salt, smoked paprika salt, citrus salt, shiso salt, rosemary salt, blended-herb salt . . . the list goes on and on. And I'm always trying to discover new salt combinations.

There are essentially three types of culinary salt: iodized table salt, kosher salt, and sea salt. Some distinguish a fourth type, fleur de sel, but it's really just a kind of sea salt, so we'll make do with the three.

I find table salt unsatisfactory on a number of levels. It contains additives that make it pour easily no matter how humid the weather. It also tends to melt and go into solution in a general sense, salting the dish in toto, but somehow doing this unpleasantly to my taste. It makes foods taste processed. Worst of all, it contains iodine, a taste that lingers in my neurons from childhood cuts and scrapes, on which my mother slathered the vile orange stuff. If salt gives even a whiff of this scent—and iodized salt does—it does not belong on food.

Kosher salt is harvested the same way table salt is—by shooting pressurized water into salt deposits, capturing and evaporating that solution, and then collecting the salt crystals that remain—but kosher salt crystals are then raked, which gives them a much larger crystalline structure. These larger crystals absorb blood from slaughtered animals better than table salt does. Because Jewish dietary laws require blood to be extracted from meat before it is eaten—a process called *koshering*—it became kosher salt. It contains none of the additives of table salt.

Sea salt is simply evaporated seawater. It contains all kinds of trace ingredients, is generally less dense than table salt, and tastes like the ocean.

I've done my share of blind salt tastings on finished food, and the results have been overwhelmingly conclusive: sea salt makes food taste better. Part of the attraction seems to be the trace amounts of other sea stuff that cling to it (notes of seaweed, maybe, or just a general "oceany" feel to it). But another major benefit is textural: the larger, crunchier crystals provide localized salt bursts that make food wake up and shine in the mouth. Larger crystals resting atop the finished food remain separate components, not unlike an herb or a piece of citrus zest.

I use kosher salt in the beginning stages of cooking: for seasoning sautéed shallots and onions, on meat, fish, and chicken, whenever salt is needed during the cooking process. It lacks the mineral notes of sea salt, but the oversized crystals are good for pinching with your fingers; they fall on food like little snowflakes. Because kosher salt has a surface volume many times larger than table salt, it doesn't taste as "salty" as normal compact table salt does. It's tasty, easy to work with, and cheap: you can get a large box for a dollar or two.

Once food is cooked or ready to be served, I use sea salt. I keep two small ceramic bowls of it next to my stove. One is sel gris, the gray, large-crystal salt from Brittany, which tends to be moister than other salt. The other is a whiter, Mexican sea salt that has smaller crystals and doesn't taste quite as oceany. There is something satisfying and aesthetic about reaching into a bowl and pinching the exact amount you want. I never use salt shakers—the holes aren't big enough to accommodate the salt I prefer, and I have more of a "feel" for how much salt should be used by touching it with my fingers. (To keep things simple in the recipes that follow, I don't specify the use of sea salt, but readers are encouraged to use it copiously.)

I also keep a half dozen or so blended salts near the stove, each in its own pretty little ceramic bowl; these are explained in detail on pages 36 to 37. These salts can turn the most ordinary of dishes—poached eggs, tofu, grilled chicken, corn on the cob—into sublime taste sensations with no work other than simply pinching some and sprinkling it on.

If you take away just one thing from this book, let it be this: good salt is your friend. It can elevate your cooking from the predictable and mundane into something lofty and invigorating.

Pepper

Nothing will kill a dish faster or more thoroughly than stale preground pepper. Whole peppercorns, to be ground as needed, make a tremendous difference in your cooking.

Many people grind their peppercorns at the time of use, with a pepper mill. There is nothing wrong with that, but I find the required two-handed motion a nuisance. Not only do I have to drop what I'm doing with my other hand, but I usually need at least ten cranks of the thing to get the amount I want.

I grind mine in a small electric coffee mill that is a dedicated spice grinder. I pour the ground pepper into yet another small ceramic bowl that sits right next to my salt. As with the salt, I reach in with my fingers and grab whatever amount of pepper I need. It's faster and more accurate than grinding and requires only one hand. I grind enough pepper for about three or four days of use. I also like to pulse the peppercorns so that some of them remain coarser than others. Finely ground peppercorns are not as aesthetically pleasing as pepper that varies in its coarseness; some of the peppercorns will be barely crushed, while the pepper in other parts of the bowl will be finely ground. A pinch with your fingers will typically pick up both.

I sometimes use pink and green peppercorns, and even a blend of all three, but they have not yet graduated to always-by-the-stove bowl status. I don't use white peppercorns—the smell of them is offputting to me, even if a dish might be more visually appealing with it.

I am quite generous with my use of both salt and pepper. I find that most home cooks underuse both. Many seem unaware that the pleasure in eating great restaurant food comes from the liberal use of salt (and butter, of course). Start on the conservative side and add more until it tastes right.

Breakaway Equipment

I am not a believer in "sets" of cookware. Some of the set is useful, and much of it isn't. Why own something that doesn't get used and just takes up valuable space? Buy your cookware as you need it, one piece at a time. Kitchens that have disparate cookware are homier and have more character than a long row of matching cookware. Avoid matching sets of all kinds, be it tableware, sheets, furniture, or cookware. There is great beauty and intimacy in asymmetry.

This is what I have in my kitchen:

Blender

The blender is the appliance used most frequently in my kitchen. Inexpensive blenders work fine for many, if not most, jobs, but I find a more powerful blender to be a pure joy to use. I use the mighty Vita-Prep, which packs a remarkable two-horsepower motor. It makes a fine powder out of whole grains without even pausing for breath and will puree anything. It also has a dial for variable speed, a function I've grown fond of over the years, because I always start out slow and increase to whatever speed is called for.

Chef's Pan

A chef's pan is essentially a small wok, about 10 inches in diameter, with a handle, but I find it superior to a wok because of its smaller size, its flat bottom, and its surface, which resists sticking (at least the one I have, made by Calphalon), thus obviating the need for excessive oil. It does a magnificent job cooking vegetables, fried rice, and dozens of other foods.

Clay Pots

Chinese, Japanese, and Southeast Asian markets carry these useful and pretty yet inexpensive things. Even Emile Henry, the French maker of ceramicware, has started to make clay pots. They can be used for hot pots, as casserole dishes, or even on the stovetop (good for browning meat—the heavier ones are effective over high heat for searing—then putting them in the oven with some liquid for braising). They can also be set on the table as is (using a trivet, of course) for a rustic presentation. I have three sizes: small, medium, and large.

Dutch Oven

The Dutch oven is essentially a braising pan. It's perfect for cuts of meat that require the slow, moist heat of a braise, especially larger cuts like pork butt/shoulder or beef chuck, blade steak, or round. Quality really matters here; mine is made by All-Clad.

Egg Pan

Egg proteins have some of the nastiest sticking properties around. Assuming you're an egg fan, as I am, and eat a lot of them, you should dedicate a nonstick pan to eggs only; it will continue to perform beautifully for years. I prefer the Le Creuset 10-inch nonstick enameled cast-iron pan, which is significantly heavier than other nonstick pans.

Knives

Again, you don't need a "set" of knives. Just three or four well-chosen and comfortable knives, possibly from different makers, are plenty. If you ask people with a fancy set of knives which ones they actually use, the answer will almost invariably be just two or three.

The most daunting part of cooking for a lot of people seems to be related to knives. I've found that my enjoyment of cooking is directly proportional to the quality and sharpness of knives: the sharper they are, the more I enjoy them (and conversely: dull knives are no fun at all). Cutting vegetables and especially meat becomes tiresome if the knife works against you rather than for you.

My main workhorse is a six-inch chef's knife, but I also make heavy use of a paring knife. I use both Henckel and Wüsthof, but the maker matters less than comfort and heft, the feel of the knife in your hand. It must be comfortable. Also on hand in my kitchen are a Japanese vegetable cleaver (good for large jobs that involve lengthy periods of chopping) and a long, serrated bread knife. These are the knives I use on a daily basis.

Great meals can, of course, be made with cheap knives—actually, this goes for all kinds of cheap cookware—but after one has risen to this challenge, why continue? Cheap crap, as the iconoclastic food writer John Thorne once wrote, is never neutral: "It constantly drags at your self-respect by demeaning the job at hand."

Pasta/Soup Pot

Pasta likes being cooked in plenty of water, so it's important to have a big pot. Also handy for making large quantities of soup, for brining whole chickens, and for use as a large vessel into which one can dump just about anything. Quality is less important for this pot than for any of the others, but avoid the cheap aluminum kinds.

Roasting Pan with a Rack

Essential for roasting whole chickens, turkeys, and many other things. I like it for cooking bacon in the oven. When meats are on a rack, the fat renders (melts) and drips below into the pan. I often line mine with a sheet of aluminum foil to facilitate cleanup. Make sure the pan will fit into your oven before purchasing!

Saucepans

You might like a small nonstick saucepan for things like making oatmeal, small quantities of rice and soup, and simple sauces. A medium saucepan, again nonstick, is good for rice, soup, and reheating. Both should have tight-fitting lids.

Skillets, Small Nonstick

I keep two of these hanging around for smaller jobs such as sautéing shallots or onions, making simple sauces, and frying small quantities of anything.

Skillet, Stainless, 10-inch, Oven-Safe

This is essential for browning/searing meats, which need to be finished in the oven to make sure their middles are sufficiently cooked. Also good for braising, provided you have a tight-fitting lid for it.

Spice Grinder

A small, inexpensive electric coffee mill is the ideal tool for grinding spices. You can grind pepper to the desired consistency in no time. It's especially good for making quick work of whole dried spices and grains such as star anise, coriander seeds, lentils, and rice flakes (for making crusts) and for making bread crumbs from stale bread. It's also essential for making flavored salts (page 36). A spice grinder is one of the best twenty-dollar investments you can possibly make.

Zesters

These wonderful little tools—based on the design of the rasp, the woodworking tool designed to shave wood—will greatly expand the range of your cooking. They efficiently remove the zest (the colored skin) from any citrus fruit, which can then be used as is or chopped up in any number of shapes and sizes. Many of the recipes in this book use zest, and this is the tool best designed to remove it. You can use a knife to peel zest off, but it's time-consuming, wasteful, and messy. With a rasp zester you can zest a lemon or an orange in about 10 seconds. I use three kinds: (1) the five-hole one for long strands of zest; (2) the Microplane fine, which makes zest so fine it almost begins to take the form of liquid; and (3) the Microplane coarse, which makes short work of a recalcitrant chunk of Parmesan or other hard cheese, stale bread, cucumbers, potatoes . . . its list of uses goes on and on.

The Breakaway Pantry

It took me a long time to realize that cooking is vastly more enjoyable and creative if your pantry is filled with fresh and varied products. Like many people, I used to keep stuff in my pantry that was, shall we say charitably, well past its prime. My golden rules now are:

- Keep quantities small and manageable.
- Keep everything visible—it's too easy to forget about things you can't see.
- Use *everything*; don't let things sit around.

The better managed your pantry, the more comfortable you become with key ingredients. And the better, more interesting cook you become.

The first thing to do is throw out as much as you can possibly bear, especially rancid oils. If oil tastes or smells off in any way (especially if it smells like motor oil), it is rancid. There is no way to get through this mildly unpleasant task other than to just do it, item by item. Every single thing in your pantry should be examined. With the exception of canned goods and a few spices (more on those below), if they haven't been used in six months to a year, the likelihood of using them in the immediate future is low. So throw them out! For this exercise/exorcise, it is better to err on the side of abandon (if even *slightly* in doubt, throw it out) than frugality.

The most basic of pantries stocked with just a few key ingredients can provide delicious meals in less than thirty minutes—often much less—even when you haven't gone shopping in a while and there is next to nothing in your refrigerator. Having a kitchen stocked with very basic ingredients is liberating. You'll be confident that you can feed an unexpected guest or two, no matter how long it's been since you last went shopping.

Think of your necessary items as belonging to two groups: perishables and nonperishables. My refrigerator is pretty small, so I can't stock it as well as I'd like to, but at a minimum I almost always have the following:

- fresh eggs
- tofu
- unsalted butter
- miso
- fresh ginger
- Greek yogurt (I like Total yogurt)
- mustard
- carrot juice
- jam
- maple syrup
- yuzu juice
- chutney
- fresh herbs
- Garlic Confit (page 41)

The list is a bit longer for nonperishable items. I don't have much pantry space, but I am always supplied with:

- fruity extra virgin olive oil (usually at least three kinds)
- vinegars: balsamic, rice, brown rice, champagne, red wine, sherry, and usually a few homemade fruit vinegars, like fig, cherry, and persimmon (made by pouring champagne vinegar into a clean jar, adding chopped dried fruit, and allowing it to macerate for a few weeks)
- soy sauce
- citrus fruit of all kinds
- whole dried spices, especially star anise, black and green peppercorns, coriander seeds, fennel seeds, and chipotle chiles
- sweeteners: honey, light brown sugar, dark brown sugar

- pasta: as many kinds as possible
- rice: white and brown, short-grain and long-grain
- potatoes
- onions, yellow and red
- shallots
- nuts: almonds, cashews, pine nuts, walnuts, peanuts
- salts (page 36)

That's really about it. The most important thing is to be sure that all ingredients are fresh. The more frequently you cook, the fresher everything will be. Buy small quantities. This is especially important with olive oils. If a bottle of oil doesn't smell fruity and delicious, throw it out and get another one.

A number of key global "flavor blasts" are used repeatedly throughout this book. They are very easy to gather and have lying around in your fridge and pantry. See pages 35 to 48 to find out more about these ingredients.

Breakaway Tastes

Tangy: Citrus Juice and Vinegars

Citrus juices and their zests play a central role in my daily cooking. Just a few drops from a lemon, especially if it's a Meyer lemon, is an immediate wake-up call on my palate.

If I detect no sourness or acidity in a certain food, I'm likely to want to add some, through the addition of either citrus or vinegar. The strong presence of the tangy is a—perhaps *the*—central tenet of breakaway cooking. A dish has to contain an element of acidity that I can taste and savor. The recipes throughout the book may appear wildly different in many aspects, but they all contain this central backbone characteristic of acidity, ranging from mild to intense.

I've never met a citrus I didn't like, from the common lemon to the more esoteric (and harder-to-find) Japanese citruses like yuzu and sudachi and everything in between.

As for vinegars, I typically keep (and use) about ten kinds, many of which are simply rice vinegar in mason jars infused with different fruit—figs, cherries, raspberries—as well as balsamic, champagne, sherry, brown rice, apple cider, and whatever other else happens to catch my fancy.

Savory: Fresh Herbs and Spices

Other important breakaway ingredients are herbs, used generously, because they add fresh, grassy, green, often pungent flavor. Herbs are like gifts to any aspiring cook—just use them as is, freshly chopped, and they lend their magic to whatever they touch. In particular, mint, tarragon, cilantro, and basil will brighten pretty much anything they touch, so use them liberally when they appear with heavier, earthier foods, more sparingly when they costar with something that's already bright, say a lime-centric dish like ceviche or a vinegar-centric dish like vinegar chicken.

Fresh dried spices—and no, that is not a contradiction—also figure prominently. Throw away any dried spices you haven't used in the last six months— they will destroy whatever you're cooking—and purchase some new ones in small quantities. Keep them in a dark place in small, tightly sealed jars and keep your collection small, limiting it to whatever you actually use on a regular basis.

Sweet: Complex Sugars

Sweetness lends a certain roundness to savory dishes—it makes the other aspects of any dish come together harmoniously. The catch is that sweetness can easily be overdone; it's important to be vigilant and never let a dish—even desserts—become so laden with sweetness that it sinks the dish into sickening oblivion.

I use sweeteners of all kinds, with the exception of the most common one: refined white sugar. I find there are more interesting ways of injecting sweet notes into food than by adding white sugar to it. Not a single recipe in this book calls for it.

My preferred sweeteners are maple syrup, honey, and jam. Why not, I reason to myself, get all those other flavors that go along with it? Light maple syrup adds a woodsy feeling and layers its complex goodness on most things it touches. Honey can lend just about anything—caramel, lavender, orange blossom, mesquite— besides sweetness. And jams impart their fruity goodness to the sweetness.

Nine Global Ingredients

Carrot Juice

Whenever a dish needs some kind of liquid—if the meat I'm braising is threatening to dry out, the salad dressing I've just made is too thick, whatever I'm whirring in the blender needs some liquid to make it blend properly, the bottom of the pan has a lot of tasty caramelized brown bits that will release and boost the flavor of whatever I'm cooking with the addition of a little liquid and some spatula scraping, and in dozens of other common situations—I turn to carrot juice more than anything else.

Use carrot juice as you would stock. What would you do with stock? You'd cook risotto with it, use it in soups, thin vegetable or herb purees with it, add it to mashed potatoes, use it in pasta sauces, reduce it for use as a glaze for fish or chicken, and even make ice cream with it. I usually cook rice in carrot juice (my favored proportion is one-third carrot juice and two-thirds water).

Its powerful, clean flavors will surprise you, as will the final color of dishes that use it: they tend to be bright and vibrant, making the food even more appealing. Carrot juice is readily available at supermarkets and at Trader Joe's and Whole Foods, so there's no need to go through the ordeal of juicing carrots and then cleaning up the mess.

Crusts

Crusts, or what some call breading, offer the important texture of crunch. Many people use plain bread crumbs or flour as crusts, but when crusts are combined with herbs and spices, the crusts serve as more than just crunch deliverers: they

add another layer of taste and complexity that complements whatever is being encrusted and sends it even further along the path to gastronomic nirvana.

One of my favorite crusts is rice flakes, often labeled "thick poha" (*poha thik* or *jaada poha*)—there's a "thin" variety too—in Indian markets, where they can be purchased. They are cooked, flattened, toasted grains of rice that, when combined in a spice grinder with salt, peppercorns, and almost any other spice you can think of, make some of the crispiest crusts imaginable.

Lentils, especially pink lentils (which are often more orange in color than pink, despite their name), can be ground up and used as a breading for fish, tofu, or chicken. Lentil crusts are especially good when combined with ground coriander seeds and green peppercorns.

Try stale bread, couscous, cornmeal, chickpeas, and even cream of wheat as crusts. Almost any carbohydrate that you can grind up in a spice grinder to produce a fine powder will work as a crust. Finely chopped nuts also make fine crusts.

Ginger and Galangal

Ginger is highly valued as both a medicinal and an important food in all of Asia and, increasingly, everywhere else. It perks up food, it cuts the richness of fat-laden dishes, and it masks excessive gaminess or strong oils in meat and fish. It's equally good in desserts.

Until recently, ginger for most home cooks outside Asia meant the beige powder labeled "ginger" in their dried spice collection. Today, fresh ginger is widely available, even in most supermarkets. Select hard, heavy, young-looking ginger and avoid the lighter, wizened, more wrinkled ginger, which will be fibrous and older tasting.

I peel ginger the easy way and don't worry too much about losing a little or being wasteful. Take a knob and slice off any odd, misshapen ends, keeping the meatiest section of the knob. Then, using a paring knife, simply slice away the skin, as you would an apple, and either mince or julienne the rest, depending on your intended use for it (minced ginger will blend more wholly into whatever you're cooking, and julienned ginger will retain its shape and pungency). One of my favorite foods is pickled ginger—I eat mountains of the stuff (page 38).

Galangal is also known as Thai ginger; it's more pungent than regular ginger

and much harder to slice (and to digest, since it's so fibrous). But it's a magnificent flavor blast in soups, rice, marinades, and, especially, ice cream (page 212). Just cut up a few thin coins, throw it into whatever you're cooking, and discard when done. Galangal is widely available at Asian markets.

Habaneros

Habaneros ("from Havana") are unique in the chile world: their flavor is dominated not by the familiar earthy and peppery tones of many chiles and sweet peppers but by strong notes of tropical fruit, including passion fruit, mango, papaya, and star fruit. They are utterly delicious.

Habs contain roughly 300,000 Scoville heat units (a common measure of chile heat), A jalapeño, by comparison, has only about 8,000 Scoville units. But don't let that frighten you: as long as you're careful about removing the veins and seeds, which pack most of the heat, you can fully enjoy their many marvels.

Because habaneros are among the hottest chiles in the world, they must be handled with extreme care. Some cookbooks recommend using rubber gloves when handling habs, but I find this to be unnecessary if you follow one very simple rule: don't touch them! To avoid touching the pepper, lightly pin it down with a fork and, using a sharp paring knife, slice the pepper lengthwise down the center. Then simply excise each vein (a hab typically has three or four) by slicing both sides of it. Carefully discard all but the chunks of orange flesh that remain and mince those up. Don't touch them! Use your fork to hold the flesh still and use the knife to slice or mince them. Then use the blunt side of the knife to slide them into the pan, a bowl, a plate, or wherever you're planning on using them. Then thoroughly wash the cutting board and knife with soap and hot water. Some of the capsaicin (the stuff that makes chiles hot) may remain, depending on how thoroughly you wash your tools, so be careful. Don't touch them!

Because of its power, a single habanero goes a long way. I often slice a small piece of one up for my scrambled eggs. A whole one would add considerable punch to a pot of simmering stew, a slow-cooking pork shoulder, or a Jamaican-style jerk chicken. Its tropical overtones make it ideal for seafood, especially shrimp, either thinly sliced and eaten raw or as a component of an accompanying simple salsa made with white onion, a chopped tomato, fresh cilantro, lime juice, and salt.

Maccha

Ceremonial green tea, called *maccha* in Japan (it is sometimes spelled *matcha*)—is a brilliantly colored thick green brew whipped up with a bamboo whisk and sipped mainly during formal tea ceremonies. Maccha is made from the most valued leaves of a tea plant known as *tencha*, which is grown in shade for about a month before being picked, a process that allows the chlorophyll content to ratchet upward and thus produce the tea's luminous green hue. It is then dried and pulverized into a superfine tea powder, with a consistency similar to cornstarch. A small spoonful of bitter maccha is added to the most beautiful tea bowl one owns, hot water is added, and the mixture is whipped by hand into a surreal green, thick, foamy brew. It is normally taken with a few small pieces of exceedingly sweet candy, which is said to play off the bitterness, although I have never been a convert to this particular practice.

As with many of my more or less blind discoveries in Japan, I started buying it and experimenting with it, simply making tea at first, then starting to infuse its flavors and color into my cooking. The easiest way to use it for culinary purposes is to tap it through a strainer directly onto something sweet, especially chocolate (Maccha Truffles, page 202, and Soft Chocolate Maccha Cakes, page 206). It makes a delicious base for green tea ice cream, as people all over the world have discovered.

By combining a small spoonful of maccha to several tablespoons of sea salt and whirring it in a coffee grinder, you can make a gorgeous, deeply flavorful salt that is delightful sprinkled over poached eggs (page 96), in salads, on tofu, on a baked potato, and in dozens of other uses. Maccha also happens to be full of antioxidants and vitamin C; not only is it arrestingly lovely to look at and eat, but it's also really good for us.

Alas, all this pleasure doesn't come cheap: a small tin of it (about an ounce) will cost around $12 to $14 or more, depending on quality. The good news is that you need very little of it for recipes; I use it more frequently than most people, and it still takes me several months to go through an ounce. It's available at any Japanese market, some Chinese markets, and online at japanesegreenteaonline.com.

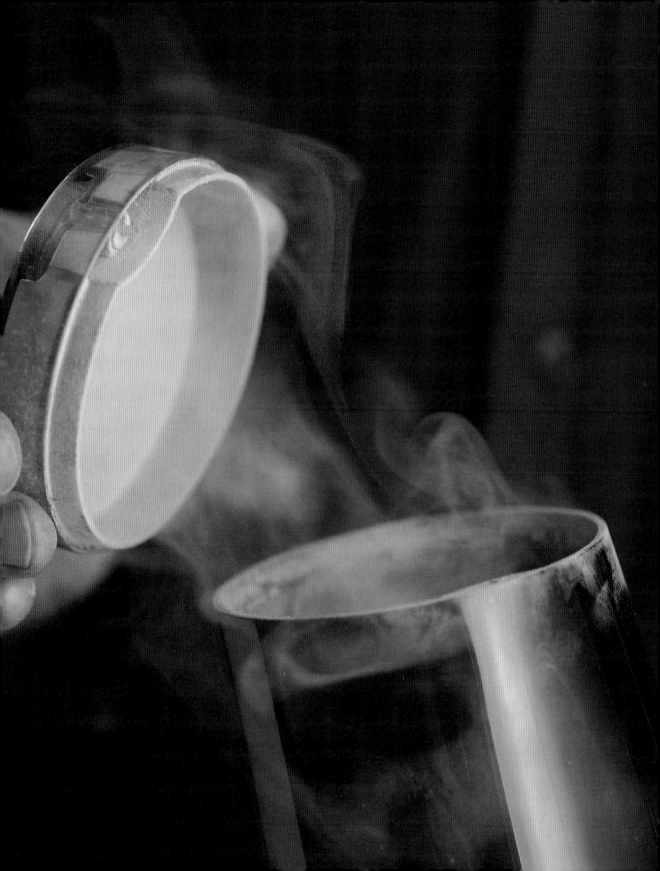

Miso

Miso has been popular in Japan for at least fourteen hundred years; Buddhist monks first brought it into Japan from China sometime in the seventh century. Its virtues are many: it's incredibly nutritious, full of protein, has little to no fat, lends deep, savory intensity to everything it comes in contact with, is easily digested, and lasts for months or even years if stored properly (tightly covered and refrigerated).

The making of miso is, in essence, a simple process: Large quantities of soybeans are first steamed, then laden with salt. Cooked grains (rice and barley are the most common) are then added, followed by a special bacterial mold known as *koji*. It then ferments for from weeks to years, depending on the desired result, in a wooden or stainless-steel tub, until ready to use. Miso comes in many varieties and colors, ranging from light yellow (the lightest and sweetest variety), to dark yellow/brown (the most typical, medium body) to reddish brown (most savory, most salty, most intense). Generally speaking, the lighter the color, the milder and sweeter the flavor. The dark yellow/brown variety is the most versatile, but I keep all three in my refrigerator at all times.

Miso soup—consumed by tens of millions of Japanese for breakfast and often for lunch and dinner too—is almost always made with dashi (a stock made from dried bonito and kelp) as a base, but it's also excellent with other stocks. The combination of chicken stock and fennel (page 80) brings out the best in miso.

Miso can also be used as a base for marinades, used in glazes for broiled fish, eaten straight with cucumber spears and beer (page 75), stuffed under the skin of a chicken before it's roasted (page 124), added to stewed pork (page 149), served on mashed potatoes as a gravy (page 169), and used in countless other ways when you need a savory blast.

Miso is now widely available, even at supermarkets. But for a better and more eclectic selection, visit a Japanese or Asian foods market.

Pomegranate Molasses

Pomegranates are not a peel-and-eat fruit like bananas. In fact, there really is no "fruit" at all, since the only edible part of the pomegranate is its seeds, which look like large bright red popcorn kernels. The seeds are quite a bit of work to remove, make a red mess everywhere, and tend to be tart. As if that weren't enough, they're challenging to eat: like half-popped popcorn, they require delicate chewing, since one can't simply chomp down on them without the risk of some major tooth damage. Used sparingly, they're best sprinkled on salads and used as a base for a fruit salsa. They lend rich color to finished dishes, but it's hard to get excited about enjoying them in the same way that most people love eating more accessible seasonal fruit.

Pomegranate molasses, sometimes called *pomegranate concentrate,* is a viscous, treacly syrup made from cooked-down pomegranate seeds that provide the intense fruit flavor without any of the labor. It has a beautiful, ruby-red color and a deliciously tart, faintly sweet flavor. It can be found in bottles for about $4 at Middle Eastern, Indian, and some Asian markets, but it's showing up with increasingly frequency at supermarkets, gourmet food stores, and other specialty markets. You can always find it at ethnicgrocer.com, among other online sources.

Pomegranate molasses is rapidly becoming a popular ingredient since it provides an instant flavor boost to everything. It makes a beautiful glaze for broiled fish or roasted chicken. It makes the perfect marinade, along with a little olive oil and rosemary, for lamb. I pour some into the blender along with some tofu and egg and then bake that concoction (page 102). I use it on hamburgers, in salad dressings, in stir-fries, and on roasted potatoes (page 168). With a little maple syrup or brown sugar, it's also excellent on waffles and pancakes. It keeps almost indefinitely in the refrigerator, but I rarely bother; I go through bottles quickly, and it just sits on my shelf next to the olive oil.

Pomegranate juice has made a comeback in recent years, thanks mainly to its highly touted antioxidant properties. If you can find only the juice and not the molasses, make your own by heating the juice and a little sweetener to taste and reducing it to about half its original volume.

Umeboshi

Umeboshi are almost always translated as "pickled plums," but they are technically apricots. Not that it matters—what makes them interesting is their ability to provide a walloping flavor boost to many dishes. They also keep in the refrigerator for months and even years at a time, always ready to give the breakaway cook an instant and delightful flavor blast.

Many Japanese families still make umeboshi at home every June. The stores sell green, unripe ume in neat little bags, which are brought home, crammed into a ceramic crock, and packed with salt. After a few weeks, red shiso (perilla) leaves are added to give the umeboshi its classic deep-red color. More salt is added, and after a month or two they're ready to be eaten as is. Some people sun-dry them for a few days to remove excess moisture. Everyone has a slightly different recipe, but essentially these delightful little flavor balls turn into supersour, salty pieces of stone fruit.

For those of us who can't be bothered to make our own, Japanese and Chinese markets offer a wide variety of them. I prefer the fat, meaty, flavorful ones that come in sealed plastic tubs to the scrawnier ones, which are used mainly as a post-prandial digestive in Japan. Many Japanese feel that a meal isn't complete until a single umeboshi is eaten at the end. Pureed umeboshi can also be purchased; Japanese markets often sell it in a tube, to be squeezed out like toothpaste. The tube is undeniably convenient, but the whole plums taste better.

Japanese also swear by the health-enhancing properties of umeboshi. Many like to pour boiling water over one, for a "tea" that is said to reduce fatigue. Even more believe in the power of umeboshi to fight colds and to alleviate nausea. Japanese partiers swear it cures hangovers like nothing else.

All of that aside, I eat umeboshi in large quantities because of their unique taste, which might be described as a combination of sour, salt, sweet, and fruit, all in one. Using your fingers, separate the flesh from the pit (which is discarded). Chop up the umeboshi and add them directly to dishes or throw them into the blender with other ingredients like olive oil for a salad dressing or a marinade. They go especially well with duck—their tartness seems to cut right through fat—and a few flecks of them are brilliant on grilled fish or scallops. Or float an umeboshi in a glass of ice-cold vodka.

Yuzu

A yuzu is about the size of a tangerine and has a yellow-orange rind. The mature fruit produces little juice and is most highly prized for its fragrant and floral zest, which combines the best flavors of lemon, mandarin orange, and grapefruit. The unripe fruit, with its green rind, does provide some juice, which is exceedingly sour yet delicious.

It's almost impossible to find fresh yuzu outside Japan, but bottled 100 percent yuzu juice—which is almost as good and certainly more convenient—is becoming widely available at Asian markets, especially Japanese markets. A ten-ounce bottle costs around $12, but it will last a long time. Yuzu powder—dehydrated and pulverized yuzu zest—is also becoming easier to find. Searching the Internet for "yuzu juice" will yield a list of online purveyors.

In Japan, yuzu zest is used mainly to accent cooked vegetables, hot pots, custards, and fish, and it's sometimes added to miso and to vinegar to infuse them with floral notes. Juice from green yuzu is often mixed with soy sauce to form a dipping sauce known as *ponzu*.

Use a teaspoon or so of yuzu juice—its flavor is quite intense—in braising liquids for fish and vegetables or try combining it with some raw tuna and eat it spooned over good bread (page 65). Yuzu juice is also delightful mixed into a spoonful of miso and then spread on fish and broiled. Or try a few drops (or more) in a salad dressing along with some good olive oil, yogurt, and maple syrup.

Breakaway Flavor Blasts

The recipes in this section can be thought of as "breakaway flavor blasts"—building blocks that can be used when cooking. I keep most of these flavor blasts on hand so I can make quick, lively meals in minutes. Most of them remain fresh for months, so you won't have to make them very often. I encourage you to try them all at least once and to turn to them often when thinking about what to make for dinner.

Five Flavored Salts

Maccha, Tangerine, Lavender, Smoked Paprika, Kaffir Lime

Makes 2 ounces flavored salt

Using flavored salts—I also call them *finishing salts*—in your everyday cooking is the simplest thing you can do to elevate an ordinary meal into something sublime. You will still need kosher salt and sea salt, but it's useful to keep a fresh supply of these flavored salts within easy reach. If your salts are visible and near the stove, you'll reach for them often. I keep all five in small pretty ceramic bowls on my stove. If you live in a humid climate and are concerned about the salts clumping together, store them in small glass jars. Unique, flavor-packed salts are an easy pathway to instant breakaway food— they infuse their deep flavors into and impart their lovely colors to everything they touch. Try them on poached eggs, baked potatoes, grilled fish, corn on the cob, tofu, simple pastas, chicken, salad greens, fried rice, hamburgers, roasted vegetables—any finished food that you would season with plain salt. Place a small pile on each serving plate so guests can salt their own food.

These salts can be made in about thirty seconds. Combine ¼ cup sel gris or other coarse sea salt and 1 teaspoon flavor ingredient (for the Kaffir lime salt, use 2 medium Kaffir lime leaves; I keep a small bag of them in my freezer). My current favorites are:

MACCHA SALT: Powdered green tea plus salt. The stunning color bestows an ethereal beauty on foods. The slightly bitter tea marries beautifully with egg yolks, tofu, onions, and even chocolate. Read about maccha on page 26.

TANGERINE SALT: Dried pieces of tangerine (or orange) plus salt. Adds tangy, fruity, citrus notes to food. Try it sprinkled on roasted chicken, vegetable side dishes (especially beets), light pastas, shrimp, grilled fish, and omelets.

LAVENDER SALT: Dried lavender buds plus salt. Excellent on lamb (both as a salt rub before cooking and as a sprinkling afterward), salad greens, heirloom tomatoes, and avocados. Adds a floral, herbaceous touch.

SMOKED PAPRIKA SALT: Smoked, finely powdered paprika and salt. Use it when you want a smoky, powerful, earthy blast of flavor. Great on potatoes, fried rice, and grilled meats.

KAFFIR LIME SALT: Leaves of the Kaffir lime tree plus salt. This salt infuses a Thai-like flowery headiness into dishes. Works well on poached eggs, seafood, corn on the cob, and steamed rice.

◈ Pickled Ginger

Makes 1 cup ginger and 1 cup flavored vinegar

Japanese sushi restaurants serve pickled ginger in a small mound next to the fish. It serves as a palate cleanser between bites of fish—it's a great neutralizer of fish oils (and of any oil, in fact). *Gari*, as it's known in Japan, is made with rice vinegar and white sugar, but I make my own with more interesting vinegars—especially fruit-based ones such as persimmon, cherry, raspberry, and fig, but also balsamic and wine vinegars—combined with sweeteners like honey, maple syrup, and even jam. Mature ginger will work, but the young variety is superior for flavor and freshness. Look for vibrantly pink and plump ginger and avoid ginger that looks withered and tired.

Pickled ginger is excellent when served with grilled meat and fish; try a slice between bites. It's also good julienned and sprinkled on salads. And you can use the leftover ginger-infused vinegar as you would any vinegar—in vinaigrettes, as part of a sauce, on fish. You can use it immediately, but the flavors get even better with time.

To prepare the ginger, peel it, then slice it with a mandoline or Benriner slicer or, if your knife skills are good, a sharp knife.

The formula is easy to remember: 1 part ginger, 1 part vinegar, and a touch of sweetener (to taste). Here's one example.

1 cup very thinly sliced baby ginger
1 cup flavored vinegar, such as fig, plum, red wine, or raspberry
2 tablespoons honey

Bring 2 cups water to a boil in a small saucepan, add the sliced ginger, and blanch for 2 minutes. Drain and transfer the ginger to a container with a tight-fitting lid.

In the same saucepan, heat the vinegar and honey until it barely simmers; stir. Pour the vinegar mixture over the ginger. Cover tightly and refrigerate. Keeps for at least 6 months.

Ume-Pickled Fennel

Makes 3 cups pickled fennel and 2 cups pickling liquid

There are many reasons to seek out umeshu (plum wine) and umeboshi (pickled plums), and this dish is a prime one. It takes just a few minutes to put together, and one taste (and look—the pinkish hue is gorgeous) tends to make everyone who tries it a die-hard fan. Serve it with grilled fish or meats for a crunchy counterpart or sprinkle it on salads to add zing. Use any leftover liquid in salad dressings or on the tofu on page 106.

Some of the plum wine for sale at Japanese markets contains whole plums at the bottom of the bottle; these tend to have the "plummiest" taste and are a good choice for this recipe.

1 cup umeshu (plum wine)

5 meaty umeboshi, pitted and roughly chopped (about ¼ cup)

1 cup rice vinegar

2 tablespoons orange blossom or other honey

1 large fennel bulb, stalks removed, sliced as thinly as possible (about 3 cups)

Combine the wine, pickled plums, vinegar, and honey in a blender and puree. Place the fennel slices in a large bowl, pour in the liquid, and cover tightly. You can eat it right away, but the flavors only get better after a few days in the fridge. Keeps for several months.

◈ Garlic Confit

Poached garlic, or garlic confit (*confit* refers to cooked food that is covered in fat of some kind, serving as both a seal and a preservative), is mellower than raw garlic yet provides plenty of garlicky goodness. I keep a mason jar of it, barely covered with oil, in the fridge. Whenever I need garlic, I open the jar and spoon out a few cloves (or more). I often use a spoonful of the garlic-infused oil too. Use the confit as you would fresh garlic.

Many markets now sell small bags of already-peeled fresh garlic, and this is what you want for your confit, unless you don't mind peeling the three or four heads of garlic required for this recipe. Just be sure to make your confit as soon as you buy your bag of unpeeled garlic, because the window of freshness on peeled garlic is short. Don't buy peeled garlic that has brown spots or looks even slightly slimy—only use the plump, vibrant, healthy-looking garlic.

About 50 garlic cloves, peeled
Enough canola oil to cover them in a small saucepan

Slice off the brown root end of each clove and place the cloves in a saucepan. Cover them completely with the oil. Heat the oil very, very gently—you want bubbles to rise but not break the surface. Slow and gentle is the key here. Cook for about 40 minutes, stirring occasionally. Turn off the heat and let the cloves cool in the pan. Then transfer to a lidded jar and refrigerate. The confit will last in the refrigerator, sealed and in oil, for a few months, but you will go through it quickly once you taste how good it is and start using it regularly.

◈ Plum-Ginger Chutney

Makes 1 cup

Try this chutney with grilled meats; it's especially good on hamburgers. It's perfect with pork tenderloin, eggs, and even on toast for a quick snack.

1 tablespoon unsalted butter
¼ cup finely minced shallot or red onion
1 tablespoon minced peeled fresh ginger
4 fresh plums (any kind), peeled, pitted, and chopped
¼ cup umeshu (plum wine)

Melt the butter in a small saucepan over medium heat, add the shallot and ginger, cook for a minute, then add the plums. Turn up the heat, add the plum wine, and bring to a vigorous boil. Reduce the heat slightly and continue cooking for about 10 minutes, stirring often. Let cool a bit, then transfer to a lidded jar or plastic container and refrigerate. Keeps for 2 weeks.

◈ Breakaway Croutons

Makes 1 cup

Croutons take only a few minutes to make, and they taste so much better than store-bought ones, plus you get the satisfaction of using up old stale bread. Almighty star anise and coriander give off incredible aromas as the croutons crisp up. Float them on top of soups or sprinkle them into salads.

1 teaspoon unsalted butter
1 teaspoon extra virgin olive oil
1 teaspoon freshly ground star anise
1 teaspoon freshly ground black pepper
½ teaspoon freshly ground coriander
1 cup ¼-inch cubes stale sourdough or other bread
Healthy pinch of kosher salt

Melt the butter with the olive oil in a small skillet over low heat. Add the spices, which will foam up a bit. Let them cook for about 1 minute, until very fragrant. Add the bread, increase the heat to medium, and cook, shaking the pan frequently to prevent burning, until the croutons are crisp, about 5 minutes. Season with salt. You'll probably use them all up immediately, but store any leftovers in a small jar. Keeps refrigerated for up to 1 week.

◈ Lemongrass Citrus Syrup

Makes 1½ cups

This powerful seasoning bursting with citrus flavor is to be used wherever a combination of savory and sweet is required. It, along with maple syrup and honey, is one of my favorite sweeteners, and I always keep a jar in the fridge. It's easy to make and will keep for months, just like maple syrup. Use it in salad dressings, in meat and fish glazes, on pancakes, in barbecue marinades, over yogurt . . . its uses seem endless. Tweak the sweetness level with more or less honey.

1 quart orange juice
Juice of 1 lemon
Juice of 1 lime
2 lemongrass stalks, roughly chopped
Pinch of cayenne
2 tablespoons honey
1 tablespoon coarsely chopped peeled fresh ginger
Pinch of kosher salt

Put all the ingredients in a medium nonreactive saucepan and bring to a boil. Turn down the heat and simmer for 1 hour. Strain, cool, pour into a glass jar with a tight-fitting lid, and refrigerate for up to 3 months.

◈ Chipotle Sauce

Makes about 2½ cups

The smoky, spicy goodness of a tiny can of chipotle chiles (dried and smoked jalapeños) in adobo sauce is pure delight. It's awfully fiery on its own, though, so I temper it with a can of tomatoes and then perk it up with a little lime. In just a few minutes you'll have an excellent base for broiling fish, a sauce for poached or scrambled eggs, a flavor boost for fried rice, and dozens of other uses for which a deep, smoky burst of spicy flavor is needed. You can find chipotle in adobo at Mexican markets or online, though many supermarkets also carry it.

One 7-ounce can chipotle chiles in adobo
One 14-ounce can diced tomatoes, preferably organic
Zest and juice of 1 lime
Kosher salt

Combine the chipotles with the adobo, tomatoes with their juice, the grated zest and juice of the lime, and salt to taste in a blender. Puree and transfer to a glass jar with a tight-fitting lid. Keeps in the refrigerator for 3 weeks.

Basil-Lemon Sauce

Makes about ²/₃ cup

Now that fresh basil is available year-round, I use this sauce all the time. Try it on salads, on eggs, on cooked vegetables, and over grilled fish. Regular lemons can also be used.

10 large fresh basil leaves (about 1 cup loosely packed)
Zest and juice of 2 lemons, preferably Meyer
½ cup fruity extra virgin olive oil
1 tablespoon maple syrup

Combine the basil, lemon zest and juice, oil, and maple syrup in a blender. Puree and transfer to a jar with a tight-fitting lid. Keeps in the refrigerator for about 7 to 10 days.

◈ Crispy Ginger Topping

This versatile topping adds crispy goodness when sprinkled on barbecued meats, grilled fish, and even soft tofu. Make a lovely breakfast jam out of it by adding sweetener (honey is best) and enjoying it on your morning toast.

1 tablespoon unsalted butter
1 tablespoon extra virgin olive oil
1 tablespoon rice flakes
Pinch of kosher or other salt
Pinch of freshly ground black pepper
½ cup julienned peeled ginger

Melt the butter with the olive oil in a small skillet over low heat. Combine the rice flakes, salt, and pepper in a spice grinder and grind until you have a fine powder. Toss the rice flakes with the ginger in a bowl.

Raise the heat to medium-high and sauté the ginger mixture for about 5 minutes or until as crisp as desired. Drain on paper towels and salt to taste.

Breakaway Beverages

Wine

Food makes wine taste better, and wine makes food taste better. The alchemy can be almost transcendental.

But how does one go about selecting something for dinner amid a mind-boggling array of choices? The only real way is to start tasting some of them. The old rule of thumb—white with lighter food, red with heavier food—is a good place to start. What you're looking for is synergy. You don't want wine and food just to tolerate each other: each should enhance the other while preserving the fundamental character and uniqueness of both. And there's really only one way to figure this out: taste the food, taste the wine, and then taste them together.

Here are a few things to keep in mind:

- For a dinner that involves more than one kind of wine, serve lighter-alcohol wines first and proceed with increasingly higher-alcohol wines.
- Champagne and sparkling wines go with just about everything (except rare red meats). Whenever you're stumped about a pairing, try a sparkler.
- Consider wine as a "sauce" or condiment for your dish. If you're having a shrimp cocktail or a ceviche, what would taste good as a sauce? Probably something citrusy and herby. For that, you'd go with a Sauvignon Blanc or perhaps a Pinot Grigio. Like butter on your lobster? Then a big buttery oaky Napa Chardonnay would fit that bill. If you're having salmon barbecued on a wood plank, you might want something a little smoky and peppery and silky with it, like a Pinot Noir. A grilled piece

of marinated venison might call for a gutsy, "gamier" wine like a Zinfandel.

- Sweeter wines are like dessert. In fact, more often than not, they are my dessert. Serve them for the conclusion of the meal.
- Whatever you do, don't fret over the "perfect" pairing, which in fact has little to do with wine: the ideal match is people you care about, a simple meal prepared with love, and a bottle of wine.

Sake

Sake, Japan's contribution to boozy gastronomy, makes a lovely accompaniment to many of the dishes in this book. Like wine, sake runs the full quality gamut, from rotgut (usually served warmed) to rare, artisanal sake (usually served chilled). Twenty years ago people outside Japan were limited to industrial plonk, but today it's easy to find quality sake (for a comprehensive inventory and plenty of well-organized information on sake, take a look at truesake.com).

Sake is the fermented result of the ancient practice of combining steamed rice, water, yeast, and a starch-dissolving mold known as *koji*. Most sakes have an alcohol content around 16 percent.

For our purposes, think of sake as being comprised of three basic grades, even though, technically, there are more. The grades are really about the degree to which rice is milled—how much of the outer portion is removed from each grain—and not about the rice "varietal" (though some would argue that rice *terroir* and water quality play huge roles). The more the rice is milled, the more refined the sake:

- Junmai—"table sake." Made from lightly milled rice. Tends to be earthy and uncomplicated.
- Ginjo—"premium sake." The rice undergoes a more refined milling, which results in complexity and lighter, drier flavor profiles.
- Daiginjo—"superpremium sake." The most milled of all sakes. This is the good stuff: daiginjos can rival the world's great wines in complexity and sheer enjoyment. You'll pay dearly for daiginjo, but it's worth an occasional splurge to experience what a delightful beverage sake can be.

Sake labels also provide what is in essence the specific gravity (a measure of how much sugar has been converted into alcohol) of the sake, expressed as a positive or negative number typically ranging from -5 to +15. Negative numbers indicate more residual sugars and thus a sweeter sake. As a general rule of thumb, the higher the number, the drier the sake will be.

For information on every aspect of sake, visit sake guru John Gauntner's site at sake-world.com.

Tea

After water, tea is the most widely consumed beverage on the planet. Green tea is the national drink of Japan—people there tend to drink five to ten cups a day. Indians and Chinese, too, drink prodigious amounts of tea. A cup of steaming green tea provides me with a perfect delivery of serenity, wakefulness, and comfort.

All tea comes from the same plant species (*Camellia sinensis*), and it's broken down into three basic types, differentiated mainly by the processing technique each undergoes:

- black—oxidized for several hours
- oolong—oxidized for less than an hour
- green—not oxidized at all

Herbal "tea" is not tea; it's just an herb or a mixture of herbs steeped in hot water. A more accurate term for this brew is *tisane*, though lots of people also refer to it as an *herbal infusion*.

On Cooking with Tea

Tea isn't just for drinking; it's also a fine ingredient to cook with. Brewed tea adds complexity and flavor to sauces and marinades. Tea provides a unique braising liquid for chicken, tofu, and vegetables and creates lovely infusions with citrus juices. Black tea leaves pulverized in a spice grinder can be combined with cinnamon, coriander seeds, peppercorns, and salt to make an exotic spice rub for fish, chicken, or pork. Floral jasmine tea leaves, ground to a fine powder, are a good base for many desserts, including biscotti (page 208). Green tea (maccha) mixed with sea salt (page 36) is good on so many things that you may keep it around as your permanent table salt, as I do. Mix maccha with confectioners' sugar and sift it over cakes, fruit tarts, or other desserts.

Starters and Salads

I often make a whole meal out of starters and salads, both at home and when ordering in restaurants, where the appetizers are usually more tantalizing than the main courses. There's something fun and stimulating about serving and eating three or four smaller dishes in succession, without a big buildup to the main. Starter dishes also make great lunches and picnic food.

◈ Galangal-Infused Dungeness Crab with Baby Greens

Serves 6 generously

Dungeness crab season in the San Francisco Bay area goes from late fall to late spring. When crab is fresh, little else is needed besides some lemon wedges and some good salt. But when I have a little extra time, I make a simple dressing with sautéed shallots, galangal, white wine, and orange juice. Champagne works well with it, as does an Austrian Grüner Veltliner.

1 tablespoon unsalted butter

1 tablespoon extra virgin olive oil

¼ cup minced shallot

½ cup roughly chopped peeled galangal

½ cup dry white wine

Juice of 2 oranges (about 1 cup)

Cooked meat from 2 Dungeness or
    other meaty crabs (about 1 pound;
    see Note)

Tangerine Salt (page 36)
    or kosher salt

Freshly ground black pepper

6 cups baby greens, chopped
    and barely dressed with a
    splash of extra virgin olive oil
    and champagne vinegar

Chopped fresh chives for garnish

Heat the butter and olive oil in a small saucepan over low heat. Add the shallot and galangal and sauté for a few minutes. Add the wine and orange juice, turn up the heat, and bring to a boil. Reduce the heat and boil gently for about 30 minutes, until reduced by more than half. Strain. You should have about ½ cup.

Place the crabmeat in a mixing bowl and add the sauce. With your fingers, gently work in the sauce and sprinkle in salt and pepper to taste. Place mounds of the dressed baby greens on plates, spoon the crab over them, sprinkle with the chives, and add a small pile of tangerine salt on the side.

NOTE: You can use live crabs, which are clearly fresher but require considerably more work—you'll need to boil them in an extra-large pot of water, then clean out the viscera, then crack them with a small hammer—than buying crabs that have already been cooked, cleaned, and cracked. The latter are far less hassle, with only the slightest degradation of freshness, and are my preferred method. Alternatively, many fish sellers (and even Whole Foods) sell prepared crabmeat. You'll pay dearly for it, and it won't be as fresh as preparing it yourself, but this is the least-hassle method.

Ahi Salad with Plum, Asian Pear, and Avocado

Serves 2 generously as lunch or 4 as a starter for a special meal

Tuna can be overcooked in the blink of an eye, but I've discovered what I consider the ideal way to cook it: by heating shallots in olive oil, adding sliced tuna, and turning off the heat. Lime juice and fruit are then added so that the tuna "cooks" in the warm fruit juice and hot shallots.

This recipe is the epitome of flexible: you can substitute just about any fruit for the Asian pear and plum (jícama is nice, as are melon and tropical fruits like Mexican papaya). Pomegranate seeds add a festive touch but can be omitted. The fresh cilantro keeps the whole coherent and even more fragrant. Try it with an unoaked Chardonnay or a Viognier.

2 tablespoons extra virgin olive oil

¼ cup finely minced shallot

Pinch of freshly ground black pepper

Pinch of Kaffir Lime Salt (page 37) or
    kosher salt

½ pound sashimi-grade tuna,
    sliced ¼ inch thick

1 teaspoon pomegranate molasses

1 Asian pear, peeled, cored, and
    cut into small chunks

1 plum, pitted and cut into small chunks

Juice of 1 large lime

½ avocado, peeled, pitted, and
    cut into small chunks

1 tablespoon pomegranate
    seeds (optional)

1 tablespoon finely chopped
    fresh cilantro

Heat the olive oil over medium heat in a heavy skillet large enough to hold all the ingredients. Add the shallot, pepper, and salt and cook for a few minutes, until the shallot softens. Turn off the heat and add the tuna slices, pomegranate molasses, pear, and plum. Stir gently but thoroughly. Add the lime juice and stir.

Let the tuna mixture sit in the pan a few more minutes, stir again, and divide among individual bowls. Add the avocado to each bowl, then the pomegranate seeds, then the cilantro. Serve at room temperature or, if you prefer, slightly chilled.

Butternut-Ginger Spring Rolls

Makes 60 mouthwatering pieces

These rolls are fun to make and fun to eat. Take them to a party or potluck and you can expect many more invitations! Enlist a few friends to help you assemble them.

The squash is the main filling for the rolls, and the toppings that follow are merely suggestions. Add whatever colorful fruits, vegetables, and herbs appeal to you. The rice paper wrappers can be found at any Asian market. The ingredients can be prepped a day before you plan on serving them, but once rolled, they should be eaten within a few hours. Hard to go wrong with Champagne accompanying these, no matter what substitutions you make.

SQUASH

1 tablespoon unsalted butter

1 tablespoon extra virgin olive oil

1 large red onion, minced

½ cup minced peeled fresh ginger

Kosher salt

Freshly ground black pepper

1 medium-large butternut
    squash (about 3 pounds),
    peeled, seeded, and
    cubed (see Notes)

¼ cup fruit vinegar such as fig
    vinegar

TOPPINGS

1 pound (about 60) green beans,
    ends trimmed, steamed
    until crisp-tender

2 cups julienned fennel bulb

2 cups julienned scallion greens

2 cups shredded radicchio

2 cups chopped watercress

2 cups chopped fresh mint

¼ cup raspberry puree (see Notes)

Lavender Salt (page 36)

WRAPPERS

1 package 9-inch round Vietnamese
    or Thai rice papers (about 30)

Melt the butter with the olive oil in a chef's pan or wok over medium heat. Add the red onion, ginger, and salt and pepper to taste and sauté for about 10 minutes, until soft. Add the squash and continue to cook for 15 to 20 minutes, stirring and shaking the pan often, until it too gets very soft but still holds its shape. Add the vinegar, mix, taste for salt, and transfer to a large bowl.

Place each topping in a small bowl and set the bowl of squash, the bowls of toppings, and an extra-large bowl of warm water (big enough to accommodate the rice paper) on a large work surface. Lay out a clean dry kitchen towel nearby. Place one rice paper in the warm water, let it get soft (1 to 2 minutes) and place it on the towel. Using a second towel, blot away all remaining water. Handle the rice paper gently, since it will tear easily. Put another wrapper in the water since the assembly will take a few minutes, just the time it takes for the next one to get soft.

Place 2 green beans horizontally parallel to one another, about an inch apart, near the bottom of the rice paper circle. This will be the "frame" into which every-thing else goes. Spoon on about a tablespoon of squash between the beans, then place small amounts of fennel, scallion greens, radicchio, watercress, and mint neatly on top of and around the squash, staying within the border of the green-bean frame. Don't overstuff, or they will become unwieldy. Keep them svelte.

Begin to roll up the rice paper, starting at the bottom and keeping it as tight as possible. When you've got what seems like a tight seal over the filling, fold over the left and right sides slightly, spoon on a little streak of raspberry puree, and sprinkle on some lavender salt. Finish rolling—the rice paper should stick to itself. Continue with all 30 rolls, setting them on a baking pan as you go (after you've made one layer, place a piece of parchment paper on them and start stacking another layer of rolls on top). When you're done, slice them in half on a diagonal and arrange on a serving tray.

NOTES: Slice off the large bulbous end of the squash, where all the seeds live, and discard. Slice the remaining "log" into ½-inch wheels (you should have about 15 wheels). One by one, slice off the skin of each wheel with 7 or 8 clean cuts, leaving a kind of octagonal shape. Then cut them into long squash French fries, then cube them. You should have about 6 cups of ½-inch cubes.

To make this puree, press about ½ cup fresh raspberries through a fine sieve to separate out the seeds.

Toro-Avocado-Yuzu Crostini

Makes about 10

This is the ultimate quick but luxurious lunch or appetizer. Use the freshest of everything, especially the toro (sashimi-grade bluefin tuna belly). You can substitute almost any fish for the toro—halibut and other kinds and cuts of tuna come immediately to mind—provided it is sashimi quality. The yuzu is well worth seeking out, but you can easily substitute lemon (or, better still, Meyer lemon) and produce great results.

1 tablespoon unsalted butter

¼ cup finely minced shallot

Tangerine Salt (page 36)
    or kosher salt

Freshly ground black pepper

½ pound toro (sashimi-grade blue-
    fin tuna belly), finely chopped

1 ripe but firm avocado, peeled, pit-
    ted, and cut into ½-inch cubes

1 tablespoon extra virgin olive oil

1 tablespoon balsamic vinegar

1 tablespoon yuzu juice or
    the juice of 1 lemon

Zest of 1 lemon

1 tablespoon minced flat-leaf parsley

Thin slices lightly toasted fresh sour-
    dough or other crusty bread

Melt the butter in a small skillet over medium-low heat. Add the shallot, salt, and pepper to taste and sauté until the shallot is lightly browned and crispy, about 5 minutes. Set aside.

In a bowl, gently mix together the toro, avocado, olive oil, vinegar, and yuzu juice. Taste for salt. Top with the crispy shallots, lemon zest, and parsley. Spoon onto the bread and serve.

Edamame Salad with Pickled Ginger, Maccha Salt, and Roasted Almonds

Serves 5 or 6

The marriage of disparate textures—the creaminess of avocado, the toothiness of edamame, the give of ginger, and the crunch of almonds—works here, and the pungent pickling vinegar from the ginger infuses the whole thing with a real zing. This makes an excellent starter for any meal. Once you have all the ingredients, the salad can be assembled in just a few minutes, though it will keep well for a few hours after assembling. Try it with a sparkling Spanish cava.

1 tablespoon unsalted butter

1 tablespoon extra virgin olive oil

2 garlic cloves, minced

¼ cup minced shallot

3 cups cooked edamame (see Note)

½ cup Pickled Ginger (page 38), julienned

¼ cup vinegar from Pickled Ginger

1 avocado, peeled, pitted, and sliced into irregular shapes

Freshly crushed black pepper

Maccha Salt (page 36)

¼ cup roasted almonds, roughly chopped

Melt the butter with the olive oil in a small pan over medium-low heat. Add the garlic and shallot and sauté until soft, about 5 minutes. Transfer to a large serving bowl and add the edamame, pickled ginger, vinegar, and avocado. Mix and sprinkle in plenty of pepper. Divide the salad among individual plates, dust each serving liberally with the maccha salt, and top with the almonds.

NOTE: Follow the package instructions to cook the edamame. The frozen ones are usually boiled for about 5 minutes.

Persimmon Salad with Sweet Ginger Vinaigrette

Serves 4

I had a gigantic and prolific Fuyu persimmon tree next to my house in Japan, so I was constantly trying to figure out new ways to eat them. I turned to (and tweaked) this preparation again and again, until it became as common for me as eating a banana or an apple. Fuyus, which keep their shape, must be used here; the liquidlike Hachiyas would fall apart.

1 teaspoon unsalted butter

1 teaspoon extra virgin olive oil

¼ cup minced peeled fresh ginger

Pinch of kosher salt

Pinch of freshly ground black pepper

1 tablespoon maple syrup

1 teaspoon champagne vinegar
    or other light vinegar

3 Fuyu (flat-bottomed) persimmons,
    peeled and sliced into
    irregular shapes

1 tablespoon finely minced
    fresh mint leaves

Melt the butter with the oil in a small pan over medium heat. Add the ginger, salt, and pepper and cook for about 5 minutes. Add the maple syrup and vinegar and set aside.

Arrange the persimmon slices on 4 plates, spoon the sauce over each, and top with the mint.

◈ Spicy Corn Salad

Serves 4 generously

This salad is remarkably refreshing and satisfying, particularly in the summer when corn is at its peak. Add any vegetable you like to the salad (zucchini, green beans, and sugar snap peas are all good), but be sure that everything is diced the same size (the size of a kernel of corn). Fresh habaneros are the chile of choice, but if you can't find them, use jalapeños. The salad is also good served cold and can be made a day in advance.

1 teaspoon unsalted butter

1 teaspoon extra virgin olive oil

½ medium red onion, minced
    (about 1 cup)

1 small habanero chile, seeds and
    veins removed, minced

½ cup minced bell pepper
    (multicolored peppers
    create a nice contrast)

Tangerine Salt (page 36)
    or kosher salt

3 ears of corn, kernels sliced
    from the cob with a knife

2 tablespoons champagne vinegar

1 teaspoon maple syrup

Zest and juice of 1 lime

¼ cup minced fresh chives

2 tablespoons minced fresh cilantro

Melt the butter with the olive oil in a wok or large skillet over medium heat. Add the red onion, habanero, and bell pepper. Salt liberally and sauté for 3 minutes, until everything softens. Add the corn kernels and cook for another 3 minutes. The corn should be hot but not browned. Turn off the heat.

Add the vinegar, maple syrup, and lime zest and juice and stir. Taste for salt and transfer to a warm serving bowl. Top with the chives and cilantro.

◈ Warm Herb-Fennel Salad with Yogurt

Serves 4

This salad never fails to satisfy; the combination of fresh herbs wakes up the fennel, the marmalade adds both pungency and sweetness, and the creamy yogurt holds the whole thing together. Try it in place of your usual green salad. Goes great with a chilled glass of Viognier.

1 tablespoon unsalted butter

1 tablespoon extra virgin olive oil

1 garlic clove, thinly sliced

1 medium-large fennel bulb, stalks removed, very thinly sliced, a few fronds reserved for garnish

Tangerine Salt (page 36) or kosher salt

Freshly ground black pepper

Small splash of carrot juice, chicken stock, or water

¼ cup coarsely chopped flat-leaf parsley

¼ cup coarsely chopped fresh cilantro

¼ cup coarsely chopped fresh mint

1 tablespoon orange marmalade

2 tablespoons Greek yogurt

Melt the butter with the olive oil in a wok or large skillet over medium heat, add the garlic, and sauté for a minute, until it softens a bit. Add the fennel, tangerine salt, and pepper to taste and continue to cook for 5 minutes, until the fennel softens. Add the carrot juice and cook for another minute or so, until it disappears. Add the herbs and marmalade, sauté for another minute to mix the flavors, and add the yogurt. Mix gently and transfer to a serving bowl. Chop enough of the reserved fronds to get 1 tablespoon. Taste the salad for salt, spoon onto individual plates, and top with the fennel fronds.

Edamame Shiso Salad with Yuzu Vinaigrette

Serves 4 or 5 generously

Shelled edamame, usually sold frozen, taste every bit as good when cooked as the ones sold in the pod, which tend to be much more expensive and require more time to prepare. The herb shiso, a member of the mint family, is set off beautifully by the floral yuzu and rice vinegar; the combination seems custom-made for edamame. If you can't find shiso, substitute mint with a tiny pinch of cinnamon. Pair with a cold, crisp sake, preferably a Niigata junmai.

3 cups cooked edamame (see
    Note on page 66)
1 tablespoon yuzu or other citrus juice
5 shiso leaves, sliced into chiffonade
2 tablespoons extra virgin olive oil

1 tablespoon rice vinegar
1 tablespoon maple syrup
Kosher salt
Freshly ground black pepper
Zest of 1 lemon

Place the edamame in your prettiest ceramic bowl that will hold them with plenty of room to spare.

In a blender, mix the yuzu juice, half the shiso, the olive oil, vinegar, and maple syrup. Gently mix the vinaigrette into the edamame. Add salt and pepper liberally and add the remaining shiso. Sprinkle the lemon zest on top.

◈ Cucumber Salad

The juicy crunch and pure taste of a just-picked cucumber is a marvelous thing, but salt it to draw out most of its water and it becomes a delightful little sponge into which you can inject all kinds of flavorings. Try this recipe, then use your imagination to create new ones.

2 cucumbers, peeled, seeded, and
    grated
Kosher salt
1 teaspoon fruity extra virgin olive oil
Chopped zest and juice of ½ orange
Juice of ¼ lemon

Chopped zest of ½ lemon,
    preferably Meyer
2 tablespoons maple syrup
Small pinch of ground cinnamon
1 tablespoon minced fresh tarragon

Put the grated cukes in a strainer in the sink and salt them liberally. Allow to sit for 10 minutes. Using your hands, squeeze as much water from the cukes as you can. Place them in a bowl and add the oil, citrus juices, maple syrup, and cinnamon. Mix well. Sprinkle on the tarragon and zests and serve.

◈ Moroccan Morokyu

Morokyu is the Japanese term for a refreshing summer dish of sliced fresh cucumber dipped in miso paste and enjoyed with beer on hot, muggy days. A bit of pomegranate molasses brings a fruity tartness to the savory miso paste. The cucumbers are good with Belgian beer, especially a Trappist ale. A tray of these disappears quickly at any party. Go for the best cucumbers the farmers' market has.

2 (or more) very fresh cucumbers, peeled, seeded, and sliced
    into spears about 3 inches long and ½ inch thick
1 tablespoon yellow miso
1 teaspoon pomegranate molasses

Arrange the cucumber spears on a plate. Mix together the miso and pomegranate molasses in a small bowl and place the bowl on the plate to serve.

Soups

Some soup recipes require hours of simmering, but not the ones in this chapter. Most of these simple, nourishing soups take only fifteen or fewer minutes to whip up, making them ideal for healthful quick lunches, between-meal snacks, and easy dinners.

◈ Supergreen Wonder Soup

Serves 4 generously

You'll be eating this bright green healthful soup fifteen minutes after you start chopping the leeks. The large quantities of herbs provide floral and earthy goodness and keep the soup very light.

1 tablespoon unsalted butter

1 tablespoon extra virgin olive oil

2 medium leeks, white and light green parts, trimmed and chopped (about 4 cups)

3 tablespoons fresh thyme leaves

Generous 4-finger pinch of Maccha Salt (page 36) or kosher salt

Generous pinch of freshly ground black pepper

1 quart chicken stock

1 cup chopped fresh mint

1 cup chopped fresh cilantro

1 teaspoon chopped nasturtium flowers for garnish (optional)

Melt the butter with the olive oil in a soup pot over medium heat. Add the leeks, thyme, salt, and pepper and sauté until the leeks soften, about 5 minutes. Add the stock and bring to a boil.

Turn off the heat and transfer the soup to a blender (you may need to do this in batches; avoid overfilling the blender with hot liquids). Add the mint and cilantro to the blender and puree. Adjust the salt and pour into warmed bowls. Sprinkle on the nasturtiums if desired and serve hot.

Miso Soup with Fennel and Ginger

Serves 4

An intensely flavored chicken stock replaces traditional Japanese dashi (seaweed-bonito broth) to create this satisfying soup. Follow the recipe and strain out all the solids to achieve an elegant, heady broth, or enjoy it rustic style, which will be more like a stew.

I use a combination of red miso (the earthiest and gutsiest) and white miso (the sweetest and most refined), but it's also tasty with plain yellow miso (which is what is widely available in supermarkets) or any combination of the three.

This strained version can be savored as is, but it also lends itself to additions like chopped winter greens or cubes of soft tofu. Accompany the soup with a small bowl of steamed rice and a few slices of Ume-Pickled Fennel (page 40).

2 tablespoons unsalted butter

1 tablespoon extra virgin olive oil

1 fennel bulb, trimmed, cored, and roughly chopped

1 red onion, minced

3 heaping tablespoons minced peeled fresh ginger

1 quart chicken stock

2 heaping tablespoons white miso

1 heaping tablespoon red miso

A few tablespoons cubed soft tofu (optional)

Sprinkling of minced fresh chives (optional)

Melt the butter with the olive oil in a skillet over medium-low heat, add the fennel, red onion, and ginger, and sauté until soft, about 15 minutes. Meanwhile, bring the stock to a boil in a small soup pot over high heat. Turn the heat down to simmer gently, add the onion mixture, and simmer for about 20 minutes.

Strain and discard all solids, add the miso, and turn off the heat. Stir until the miso is fully dissolved. Add the tofu and chives if desired.

Smoky Beefy Tomato Soup

Serves 4

Canned tomatoes are often superior to the pasty red orbs that pass as fresh tomatoes, and they are always available. The imported Italian ones in particular are a blessing: they're sweet and flavorful. Smoked paprika imparts a hint of smokiness. This soup can be served piping hot, chilled, or at room temperature when it's hot and humid outside.

1 teaspoon unsalted butter

1 teaspoon extra virgin olive oil

2 medium leeks, white and light green parts, trimmed and chopped (about 4 cups)

1 teaspoon smoked paprika

Kosher salt

Freshly ground black pepper

One 16-ounce can imported tomatoes

2 cups beef stock, preferably organic

2 cups loosely packed fresh Thai basil (or Italian basil)

½ cup milk

1 tablespoon minced fresh chives

Melt the butter with the olive oil in a large soup pot over medium heat. Add the leeks, paprika, and salt and pepper to taste. Sauté, stirring often, until the leeks soften, about 10 minutes.

Add the tomatoes. Raise the heat, add the stock, and bring to a gentle boil. Simmer for 5 minutes, add the basil, and transfer to a blender (you may need to do this in batches). Puree and return to the pan. Add the milk, stir, and taste for salt. Divide among soup bowls. Top with the chives.

Spicy Ginger–French Lentil Soup

The lentils were sitting in the cupboard, as was the beef broth. I had some cooked pork shoulder—but bacon would work too—in the fridge and an open bottle of Gewürztraminer. Onion, ginger, powdered chile, and some carrot juice—staples all—sautéed together, and voilà. This soup tastes even better the next day.

1 quart beef broth, preferably organic

1½ cups dried French green lentils

1 tablespoon unsalted butter

1 tablespoon extra virgin olive oil

1 large red onion, minced

½ cup minced peeled fresh ginger

1 teaspoon chipotle or other chile powder

1 cup carrot juice

1 cup cooked pork shoulder, 1 ham hock, or 5 or 6 slices crisped bacon

2 cups Gewürztraminer or other slightly sweet white wine

Kosher salt

A heaping tablespoon Greek yogurt or plain yogurt

Bring the broth to a gentle boil in a large soup pot over high heat, add the lentils, cover, and reduce the heat to simmer. Melt the butter with the olive oil in a skillet over medium heat. Add the onion, ginger, and chile powder. Stir and sauté until soft, about 10 minutes.

Transfer the onion-ginger mixture to a blender, add the carrot juice, and puree. Add this mixture to the lentil pot, then add the pork and wine, cover, and simmer for 1½ to 2 hours, stirring occasionally. The lentils should be very tender. Taste for salt—it will need plenty. Divide among soup bowls. Add a small dollop of yogurt to each serving.

Celeriac–Star Anise Soup

Serves 4

The delicate herbal flavors of celeriac (also called celery root) are lovely, and the root isn't nearly as daunting to prepare as it looks. I cut it into ½-inch-thick wheels, slice off the skin from each wheel, and then cut it into whatever shapes I want. The star anise really brings out its floral flavors, and the spiced bread crumbs give it a most satisfying crunch.

1 tablespoon unsalted butter

2 tablespoons fruity
    extra virgin olive oil

1 tablespoon freshly ground star
    anise, plus another pinch

2 medium leeks, white and light
    green parts, trimmed and
    chopped (about 4 cups)

Generous sprinkling of kosher salt

Freshly ground black pepper

1 medium celeriac, peeled and chopped

1 quart chicken stock

½ cup diced stale bread (sourdough
    is nice)

1 tablespoon chopped fresh
    chives (optional)

Melt the butter with the olive oil in a soup pot or roomy saucepan over medium heat. Add the star anise, leeks, salt, and pepper to taste and sauté gently until the leeks soften, about 5 minutes.

Add the celeriac and continue to sauté for 5 minutes. Add the stock, bring to a boil, and simmer for 15 minutes, or until the celeriac gets soft. Add the entire contents of the pan to a blender and puree, working in batches if necessary. Return to the soup pot and keep it warm over low heat.

Pulse the bread crusts and pinch of star anise in a spice grinder a few times, until you have coarse spiced bread crumbs. Place them in a small dry skillet over medium heat and toast until crispy, 2 or 3 minutes. Ladle the soup into hot bowls (taste for salt again when you do this) and top with the spiced bread crumbs and chives.

◈ Restorative Chicken Soup

Serves 4 generously

I have yet to meet anyone who doesn't hold some special feeling for chicken soup. The ginger, garlic, and herbs make this version especially soothing when a cold makes its presence felt—you can almost feel your body respond with contented delight. But I make it just as often when I'm feeling fine. Low effort, rich payoff—my kind of soup.

1 tablespoon unsalted butter

2 tablespoons extra virgin olive oil

1 medium red onion, minced

4 cloves Garlic Confit (page 41), chopped, or 2 fresh garlic cloves, minced

3 tablespoons minced peeled fresh ginger

Tangerine Salt (page 36) or kosher salt

Freshly ground black pepper

1 quart chicken stock

10 fresh basil leaves, chopped

½ cup chopped fresh mint

Juice of ½ lemon, preferably Meyer

1 skinless boneless chicken breast, pounded to an even thickness

1 teaspoon coriander seeds, finely ground

1 cup chopped fennel bulb (optional)

Melt the butter and 1 tablespoon of the olive oil in a soup pot over medium-high heat. Add the onion, garlic, ginger, salt, and pepper to taste and sauté for about 5 minutes. Add 2 cups of the chicken stock and transfer the mixture to a blender. Add the basil, mint, and lemon juice to the blender, puree, and return the mixture to the pot. Add the other 2 cups of stock, bring to a boil, and reduce the heat to a simmer.

Meanwhile, rub the chicken breast with a few drops of the remaining olive oil, then sprinkle the coriander seeds liberally on both sides, along with some salt and pepper.

Heat the rest of the olive oil in a small skillet over high heat and add the chicken. Thoroughly brown both sides, about 3 minutes per side. Transfer to a cutting board, chop into very small pieces, and add to the soup. If you'd like some crunchy crispness, add the chopped fennel. Taste for salt and serve piping hot in large soup bowls.

◈ Pea Soup with Herbs and Leeks

Serves 4

This soup can be made in about fifteen minutes, start to finish, thanks to the overall excellence of frozen peas (contemporary freezing techniques are vastly superior to those just a generation ago). The large quantities of fresh herbs add their floral wonderfulness to the whole, joined by the savory-sweet leeks and the bright, almost fruity quality of the young peas. Eat this soup with lavash-type crackers and a glass of chilled Viognier.

1 tablespoon unsalted butter
1 tablespoon extra virgin olive oil
2 medium leeks, white and light
    green parts, trimmed and
    chopped (about 4 cups)
Lavender Salt (page 36)
Freshly crushed black pepper

1 quart chicken stock
1 cup frozen baby peas
1 cup fresh basil leaves
1 cup fresh mint leaves
½ cup Breakaway Croutons
    (page 43; optional)

Melt the butter with the olive oil in a small soup pot over medium heat. Add the leeks and salt and pepper to taste, and sauté for about 5 minutes. Add the stock, bring to a boil, and add the peas. Simmer for a few minutes, allowing the peas to cook slightly, then transfer the soup to a blender and puree, in batches if necessary. Add the basil and mint and puree again. Return the puree to the pot. Bring to a simmer, adjust the salt, ladle into warmed bowls, and add the croutons if desired.

Eggs and Tofu

Eggs and tofu are the perfect breakaway foods: they are inexpensive, they are low in calories, and, best of all, they are blank canvases that take on whatever flavors you choose. Eggs can be infused with fresh herbs and then baked, sprinkled with flavored salts, or cooked in the styles of the world's great cuisines. With eggs and tofu in my fridge at all times, I know a quick, tasty meal is just minutes away.

When eggs are very fresh, their rich, plump, deep orange yolks taste like cream, butter, meat, fruit, nuts, and vegetable, all rolled into one perfect little package. It's not easy to find great-tasting eggs, but with the recent blossoming of sustainable organic chicken farms you should be able to track down some eggs laid by chickens that actually run around and eat grass and grubs and other organic food. Seek them out, but be forewarned—once you've had them, it'll be hard to settle for anything less.

When tofu is equally fresh, it's like eating a beautiful grain salad. And the softer and creamier my tofu is, the better I like it. Supercreamy tofu, known as *oborodofu* in Japan, resembles panna cotta or custard and is sometimes called "custard" tofu in North America, where it is becoming increasingly available. Seek out this creamy version, but the "silken" variety is fine for the following recipes, too. Just try to avoid the firm and extra-firm varieties. Before using custard tofu or silken tofu, drain it thoroughly, then wrap it in a clean tea towel or paper towel to absorb as much moisture as possible until you're ready to cook.

◈ Fluffy, Herby Eggs

On a whim, I added a bit of yogurt before scrambling some eggs. To my surprise, it made them exceptionally fluffy and airy and light, as well as creamy. I now rarely scramble eggs without yogurt, especially Greek yogurt, which has a thicker, creamier consistency than regular yogurt.

Freshly minced herbs add a floral dimension that signals, for me at least, the perfect start of the day. Serve these eggs with a hearty multigrain bread, lightly toasted, and a small side of sliced fresh seasonal fruit.

1 tablespoon unsalted butter
2 tablespoons minced shallot
Generous pinch of Lavender Salt
    (page 36) or kosher salt
Generous pinch of freshly
    ground black pepper

4 large eggs, preferably organic,
    lightly beaten
2 heaping tablespoons Greek yogurt
2 tablespoons minced assorted fresh
    herbs such as mint, thyme, rose-
    mary, parsley, basil, and Thai basil

Melt the butter in a small nonstick skillet over low heat. Add the shallot, salt, and pepper and sauté until soft, about 3 minutes. Add the eggs, stir, and cook for about a minute. Add the yogurt.

Stir up the eggs with a spatula and continue to cook until barely set, 2 to 3 minutes. Add the chopped herbs and fold in gently. Taste for salt and transfer to a warmed plate.

◈ Frittata Giapponese

Serves 2 generously

It may sound odd to use umeboshi, pickled plums, in an egg dish. But the piquant umeboshi offset rich yolks in the most pleasing way, especially when accompanied by cups of green tea. And because the breakaway cook always has ginger, umeboshi, and eggs lying around, this frittata is simple to put together. No green beans? Substitute chopped asparagus or a dark leafy green like kale, chard, or spinach. Can be made a few hours ahead.

4 umeboshi, pitted and chopped (about 1 heaping tablespoon)

4 large eggs, preferably organic

1 tablespoon maple syrup

1 tablespoon unsalted butter

1 teaspoon extra virgin olive oil

3 tablespoons chopped shallot

2 tablespoons minced peeled fresh ginger

½ cup coarsely chopped green beans

Pinch of kosher salt

Pinch of freshly ground black pepper

Put the umeboshi, eggs, and maple syrup in a blender, pulse a few times, and set aside. Melt the butter with the olive oil in a medium skillet over medium-low heat. Add the shallot, ginger, and green beans and season generously with salt and pepper. Cook, stirring occasionally, until everything softens a bit, about 5 minutes.

Pour the egg mixture into the pan, lower the heat, and add a little more salt and pepper. After a few minutes, lift a corner of the frittata; when it is lightly browned, turn it over. Either flip the frittata by tossing it up with a well-aimed flick of the wrist or put a plate over the pan and turn the pan and plate over together to drop the frittata, cooked side up, onto the plate, then slide the frittata, uncooked side down, into the pan. Cook for another few minutes, until lightly browned on the bottom, taste for salt, transfer to a plate, and serve hot (though it's also good at room temperature or cold).

◈ Shirred Shiitake Eggs

Eggs, butter, mushrooms, and cheese—a simple combination that is so much more than the sum of its parts, especially when the mushrooms are dried and pulverized to a fine powder in a coffee grinder. The technique—buttering ramekins, adding some sort of sauce to the bottom, cracking eggs on that, and baking them—is versatile and simple. Try it with a little leftover pesto or other pasta sauce, tapenade, or even chutney. Great with an English muffin and a steaming cup of tea.

1 tablespoon unsalted butter, plus a little more for the ramekins

2 tablespoons plus 1 teaspoon pulverized dried shiitake (about 1 large dried shiitake)

4 large eggs, preferably organic

Kosher salt

Freshly ground black pepper

Pinch of shredded cheese, such as Gouda

1 teaspoon minced fresh chives

Preheat the oven to 375°F. Melt the butter in a small nonstick skillet over low heat and add 2 tablespoons of the shiitake powder. Cook, stirring occasionally, until the butter begins to foam up, then turn off the heat. Meanwhile, lightly butter 2 ramekins and add a pinch of shiitake powder. Tap it around as you would to butter and flour a cake pan.

Add half the butter-shiitake mixture to each ramekin and crack 2 eggs into each. Sprinkle on some salt and pepper, then dust the tops with a teaspoon of powdered shiitake. Add the cheese and bake for about 12 to 14 minutes, or until there is very little liquid movement when you shake the ramekin (use a pot holder). With a rubber spatula, carefully transfer the eggs from the ramekins to warm plates. Top with the chives.

◈ Fire-and-Earth Eggs

Beets are almost never used as a flavoring; it's even rarer to use beets as a textural counterpoint, since they are often boiled to death. But a finely diced beet, especially when sautéed in fruity olive oil with scallions, makes a superb base into which you can fold some eggs. It's the addition of a finely minced habanero chile, however, that really sends this dish flying; the beets soften the fire of the chile and absorb all of its tropical overtones. And a big bonus: by using either red, golden, or Chiogga (beautifully striated pink swirls) beets, you can vary the final color of this dazzling dish. A chilled glass of Austrian Grüner Veltliner is great here.

1 tablespoon unsalted butter

1 tablespoon extra virgin olive oil

1 medium golden, Chiogga, or red
    beet, peeled and finely minced

1 habanero chile, minced (page 25)

¼ cup minced green and white
    parts of scallion

4 large eggs, preferably organic

Splash of fruit vinegar (berry,
    fig, ginger, date, or plum,
    but not balsamic)

Coarse sea salt

Melt the butter with the oil in a large heavy nonstick skillet over medium-low heat. Add the minced beet, habanero, and scallion and cook until the beets soften but retain some of their crunch, about 10 minutes. Turn the heat down to low, add the eggs, and stir. Cook gently for a few more minutes, until the eggs have set yet are still very soft. Add a small splash of the vinegar, stir, taste, and add salt to taste. Serve with lightly toasted country bread.

◈ Maccha Poached Eggs

Serves 2

I often eat these twice a week—I just can't get enough of them. They are simplicity itself: poach eggs in your favorite manner—I have a dedicated egg poaching pan with four individual nonstick cups—and sprinkle on some maccha salt. There is something almost celestial about the fusion of the green tea and the egg yolks: it's savory, sweet, and salty all at once. Perfect in the morning with a few slices of lightly toasted sourdough bread and a strong cup of green tea.

Dab of unsalted butter for the poaching cups or 1 tablespoon vinegar
4 large eggs, preferably organic
Generous sprinkling of Maccha Salt (page 36)

Generous sprinkling of freshly ground black pepper

Butter the poaching cups if you're using a dedicated egg poacher. Or bring a pot of water to a simmer, add the vinegar, and carefully crack the eggs into the simmering water. Poach the eggs until the yolks are more or less halfway between liquid and solid, 4 or 5 minutes for both methods.

Gently turn them out on a paper towel to absorb any excess moisture. Roll them onto a warmed plate and add a few healthy pinches of maccha salt and black pepper. Eat them while still very hot.

◈ Mole Tofu with Spiced Bread Crumbs

Serves 4

Yet again, tofu provides the ultimate palette on which the breakaway cook can paint just about anything. Hard-core cooks may want to prepare mole from scratch, but the breakaway cook doesn't always want to set aside a good chunk of the weekend for that task. Many tasty prepared Mexican moles are readily available in Mexican groceries, online, and even at big supermarkets.

This dish is excellent even without the spice crust, but I find that the crunchy goodness of the crust raises the whole dish a rung. With a glass of chilled Champagne, you have quite a lunch or starter for a multicourse meal.

TOFU

1 tablespoon unsalted butter

1 medium red onion, minced

5 large tomatillos, roughly chopped (about 1 cup)

Kosher or other salt

Freshly ground black pepper

1 heaping tablespoon red mole

2 large eggs

1 block tofu, drained, wrapped in paper towels to absorb moisture, then halved

SPICED BREAD CRUMBS

1 slice stale bread (sourdough works well), toasted lightly

1 tablespoon coriander seeds

1 tablespoon ground dried Mexican chile of choice

1 tablespoon unsalted butter

1 teaspoon brown sugar

Melt the butter in a medium skillet over medium-low heat. Add the onion and tomatillos. Salt and pepper liberally and sauté for a few minutes, until the onion softens. Add the mole and continue cooking for 5 minutes, until everything is well mixed.

Put the onion mixture into a blender along with the eggs and half the tofu. Puree, then transfer to a mixing bowl. Add the other half of the tofu to the bowl and use a fork to mix everything together. Spoon the tofu mixture into a buttered clay pot or casserole dish and smooth it out as best you can with a spoon. Bake for 30 minutes.

Meanwhile, pulse the toasted bread along with the coriander seeds and chile in a coffee or spice grinder (you may need to do this in batches). You should have about ½ cup of spiced bread crumbs. Melt the butter in a small nonstick skillet over medium-low heat. Add the bread crumbs and brown sugar and cook for a few minutes, stirring or shaking occasionally, until they get crispy.

Remove the tofu from the oven when nicely browned, taste for salt, and sprinkle on the bread crumbs. Serving it at the table in the clay pot makes a nice presentation.

◈ Crispy, Tangy Tofu

Serves 4

This is a quick, tasty, and nutritious way to start a meal and one of my favorite ways to serve tofu. The top stays crispy, yet the rest absorbs the pungent citrus sauce.

Excellent with a chilled, bone-dry sake like a daiginjo (and, even better, one from Niigata Prefecture, Japan, where it tends to be citrusy and clean-tasting). It's equally good with a glass of well-chilled Champagne.

Zest and juice (about ¼ cup) of
   1 large lemon, preferably Meyer
Zest and juice of 1 orange
2 tablespoons carrot juice
1 tablespoon honey
1 tablespoon soy sauce
Pinch of cayenne
3 scant tablespoons rice flakes
   or fine dry bread crumbs

Pinch of kosher salt
Pinch of freshly crushed black pepper
1 block silken tofu, drained, then
   wrapped in paper towels
   to absorb moisture
1 egg yolk
1 generous tablespoon unsalted butter
1 teaspoon chopped fresh chives
   (optional)

Put the citrus juices into a small saucepan, add the carrot juice, honey, soy sauce, and cayenne, and bring to a boil. Reduce the heat to low and simmer while you prepare the tofu.

Put the rice flakes (or bread crumbs), salt, and pepper in a coffee or spice grinder and pulse a few times. Be sure the paper towels have absorbed as much water as possible from the tofu, then slice the tofu along its "equator," creating 2 large flattish slabs. Cut each of those in half, giving you 4 pieces. Spoon the egg yolk on one side of each piece and evenly spread the rice-flake crust over them. Heat the butter in a small nonstick skillet over medium heat and sauté the tofu, crust side down, for about 5 minutes, until nicely browned. Carefully flip the pieces over with a spatula and briefly cook the other side, about 2 minutes. Pour some of the reduced sauce into a warm plate or shallow bowl and slide the tofu into the center of the sauce, crispy side up. Top with the orange and lemon zest and the chives if desired.

Pomegranate Tofu with Pink Lentil Crust

Serves 4

Middle Eastern flavors like pomegranate and cinnamon showcase the many wonderful properties of soft tofu. I bake this in a clay pot, but any baking dish or casserole will work just fine, and individual ramekins also work beautifully. The ground pink lentils on top give it nice crunch. Try it with a glass of Muscat or Riesling.

1 block silken tofu, drained, wrapped in paper towels to absorb moisture, then halved

1 tablespoon pomegranate molasses

1 tablespoon maple syrup

1 large egg

½ teaspoon freshly ground cinnamon

Tangerine Salt (page 36) or kosher salt

Freshly ground black pepper

Speck of butter for the baking dish

¼ cup dried pink lentils, ground to a fine powder

Olive oil spray

2 tablespoons fresh mint chiffonade

1 tablespoon toasted pine nuts

Preheat the oven to 450°F. Put half the tofu, the pomegranate molasses, maple syrup, egg, cinnamon, and salt and pepper to taste into a blender and puree. Scrape the mixture into a mixing bowl, add the other half of the tofu and, using a fork, mix it to a fairly uniform texture. Butter a clay pot or baking dish or four 4-ounce ramekins, and pour the mixture into it. Top with the pulverized lentils, spray them with a little olive oil, and bake for 30 minutes, until the top turns crispy brown. Remove and top with the mint and the pine nuts. Be sure to pass some extra tangerine or coarse sea salt for guests to add at the table.

◈ Rhubarb Baked Eggs

This recipe was born, like so many others, by dearth and by hunger. I was ravenous, too lazy to go to the store, and happened to have a pile of rhubarb from my friend Lucelle's garden and not much else in my fridge. So it seemed like a good idea to combine savory (onions), sour (rhubarb), and sweet (maple syrup) in a baked egg dish. I eat this for lunch or dinner with a glass of Champagne, but it could easily be part of a stylish weekend breakfast.

1 tablespoon unsalted butter

1 tablespoon extra virgin olive oil

1 large onion, minced

Kosher salt

Freshly ground black pepper

2 cups diced rhubarb (1 medium-large stalk)

3 tablespoons maple syrup

6 large eggs, preferably organic

1 teaspoon Dijon mustard

½ cup chopped fresh chives

1 teaspoon apricot or other fruit jam

Preheat the oven to 375°F. Melt the butter with the oil in a large skillet over medium heat. Add the onion, salt and pepper generously, and cook until softened, stirring occasionally, about 5 minutes. Turn up the heat a bit, add the rhubarb, stir, and continue to cook until the rhubarb starts to dissolve, about 10 minutes. Add the maple syrup, stir, and transfer to a buttered casserole dish or clay pot. Spread it out evenly.

Put the eggs, mustard, chives, and jam in the blender, along with a pinch of salt and pepper, and blend. Pour this mixture over the rhubarb, cover tightly with foil, and bake for 25 minutes, or until the eggs are firmly set. Remove from the oven. Using a wide spatula, transfer the eggs to a large warm plate and let guests serve themselves or divide among 4 warmed plates to serve.

◈ Tofu Custard with Ume Vinegar and Maccha Salt

Serves 4

Here is a good reason to have Ume-Pickled Fennel (page 40) sitting around. The pickling liquid makes superbly piquant and beautifully colored dressings that can be used for salads, grilled fish, and, in this case, tofu. The pinkish liquid and bright green salt over the white tofu look and taste fabulous together. Once you have the ingredients handy, this can be assembled in about one minute. It's a beautiful starter to a meal. Try it with a dry rosé.

2 cups extra-soft tofu ("custard tofu")
¼ cup liquid from Ume-Pickled Fennel
Pinch of freshly ground black pepper
Maccha Salt (page 36)

Place ½ cup of the tofu in each of 4 bowls, spoon on the vinegar, dust with the pepper, and sprinkle on generous pinches of salt.

◈ Savory Ancho Baked Tofu with Star Anise Crust

Serves 4

The smoky ancho chile gives the tofu brilliant color. The vibrant flavors meld so well together and in such a pleasing texture that even hard-core carnivores often sigh with contentment after eating this dish. Most supermarkets carry ancho chile powder these days. Serve with a salad and a chilled glass of rosé.

TOFU
1 tablespoon unsalted butter, plus
    butter for the ramekins
1 tablespoon extra virgin olive oil
1 medium red onion, minced
3 garlic cloves, crushed
1 heaping teaspoon ground ancho chile
1 tablespoon marmalade of choice

1 large egg
1 block tofu, drained well and
    cut into 4 equal pieces
Generous pinch of coarse sea salt

CRUST
3 star anise, ground (about 1 teaspoon)
¼ cup diced stale crusty bread

Preheat the oven to 400°F. Melt the butter with the olive oil in a small skillet over medium-low heat. Add the onion, garlic, and ancho powder and sauté until the onion is soft, about 5 minutes. Transfer to a blender and add the marmalade, egg, one piece of the tofu, and the salt. Puree.

Pour the mixture into a mixing bowl. Add the remaining tofu and, using a fork, blend the tofu into the mixture. Butter a clay pot or four 4-ounce ramekins and spoon in the mixture. Bake for 30 minutes.

Meanwhile, make the crust: combine the freshly ground star anise and the bread in a coffee or spice grinder and grind until you have finely ground bread crumbs. When the tofu has baked for 20 minutes, remove it from the oven, sprinkle on the bread crumbs, and return to the oven for 10 minutes, until the crust becomes brown and crispy. Serve very hot.

Seafood

Fish and shellfish have some compelling things going for them: they're quick and simple to cook, they're good for us, and they're delicious. The recipes that follow take very little time and even less expertise to make, which means they're perfect for weeknights and also on weekends or special occasions as part of a more elaborate meal.

Seafood must, however, be ultrafresh; no amount of culinary magic will revive a fish past its prime. If you buy fish fillets wrapped in plastic, it's hard to tell. I suggest doing what I do: open it up and smell it. It should smell good—oceany and grassy. If you're buying it whole, look for very clear eyes and a firm body that springs back when you poke your finger into it. Make a point of chatting up your local fishmonger (if you're lucky enough to have one); one who knows how particular you are about freshness will enjoy pointing you toward the freshest of the lot, which is what you should always buy, no matter what the recipe calls for.

◈ Crispy Rock Cod in Reduced Citrus

Serves 4, with extra sauce

One of the many enticements of this dish is its versatility. You can substitute any firm-fleshed fish for the cod, including salmon, and use any kind of citrus you have on hand. The technique—crisping just one side of the fish, then laying the fish, crisp side up, in a small amount of sauce—is borrowed from noted chef Gray Kunz and is a real winner. The hard-to-find ingredient here is rice flakes, but Indian grocers carry them. They make a beautiful crust. Excellent with Champagne.

SAUCE
2 cups fresh orange juice
½ cup chopped peeled fresh ginger
Pinch of kosher salt
Pinch of cayenne
2 tablespoons maple syrup

FISH
1 egg plus 1 egg yolk, whisked together
1 heaping tablespoon flour
Pinch of kosher salt

Freshly ground black pepper
4 rock cod fillets, about 6 ounces each
½ cup rice flakes, pulsed in a
    coffee or spice grinder with
    a pinch of salt and pepper
1 tablespoon unsalted butter
2 tablespoons extra virgin olive oil
Several tablespoons chopped fresh
    chives

Combine the orange juice, ginger, salt, cayenne, and maple syrup in a small saucepan and bring to a boil. Turn down the heat and simmer to reduce by about half (until you have about 1 cup). Taste and adjust salt and sweetness.

Whisk the egg and flour until smooth and add a generous pinch of salt and pepper. Spoon this mixture onto one side of each fillet and sprinkle on the rice flakes.

Melt the butter with the olive oil in a large skillet over low heat. Add the fish, coated side down. Sauté until golden and crisp, 4 or 5 minutes. Flip the fish and cook for 2 or 3 minutes longer. Spoon about a tablespoon of the sauce onto each individual plate and place the fish, crispy side up, on each one. Top with chives.

◈ Umeboshi Scallops

The sweet richness of scallops cries out for the tart fruitiness that umeboshi (pickled plums) deliver. It's good to marinate the scallops for a few hours in the marinade, but as little as thirty minutes will still give fantastic results. Don't try this with tiny bay scallops—they emit too much moisture. Use large, meaty, sashimi-grade scallops. The lentil topping crisps up beautifully. An earthy, full-bodied sake is a nice accompaniment, but a glass of very cold Champagne fits the bill quite nicely, too.

1 pound very fresh large scallops

5 meaty umeboshi, pitted and minced, ½ teaspoon reserved

1 tablespoon extra virgin olive oil

2 tablespoons fresh orange juice

1 large egg

Generous pinch of kosher salt

Generous pinch of freshly ground black pepper

¼ cup dried pink lentils, pulverized in a spice grinder

1 tablespoon unsalted butter

1 tablespoon extra virgin olive oil

1 tablespoon minced fresh chives

Rinse and dry the scallops and place in a bowl. Pat the pickled plums, olive oil, orange juice, and egg into a blender and puree. Pour the puree over the scallops and place in the refrigerator, covered, for at least 30 minutes.

Remove the scallops from the bowl, wipe off most of the marinade from each one with your finger, and place on a clean cutting board. Salt and pepper them, then sprinkle on the lentil powder, pressing it in with your fingers to make sure it adheres evenly.

Melt the butter with the olive oil in a heavy skillet over high heat—get the fat very hot but not burning. Then add the scallops and cook until one side gets slightly browned and crisped, about 2 minutes. Turn them over, one by one, and cook on the other side for another 2 minutes. Transfer them to warm serving plates, top with the chives, and fleck in a few pieces of the reserved pickled plums.

❖ Broiled Mackerel with Soy, Lemon, and Butter

Serves 4

I was ecstatic when I discovered Norwegian mackerel fillets for sale at my local store. I used to cook saba (mackerel) several times a week when I lived in Japan. I adore its oily goodness and assertive taste, and it's always a bargain, often priced at a fraction of most other fish.

Broiling mackerel with this simple glaze is easy: you'll be eating dinner ten minutes after you begin prepping. Try this glaze on other fish, too. Great with a bowl of steamed rice, a vegetable side dish, and perhaps a small mound of Pickled Ginger (page 38). A glass of cold, clean, dry sake will round out the meal nicely.

1 tablespoon soy sauce
1 tablespoon lemon juice, preferably
    from a Meyer lemon, plus a
    little for serving (optional)
1 teaspoon unsalted butter, melted
1 teaspoon maple syrup

Four 6-ounce mackerel fillets,
    rinsed and dried
Freshly ground black pepper
Tangerine Salt (page 36) or kosher salt
Zest of 1 lemon, preferably Meyer

Preheat the broiler. Put the soy sauce, lemon juice, butter, and maple syrup into a small saucepan over medium heat and whisk until it begins to thicken a little, about 3 minutes. Spoon this mixture onto the fillets and dust with black pepper to taste.

Broil until the surface turns brown and crispy, about 5 minutes. Turn the fillets over, then broil the other side until it, too, turns brown and crispy. Transfer to plates, taste for salt, and top with the lemon zest and, if you prefer, one more squeeze of lemon.

Pomegranate-Glazed Salmon

Serves 4

Pomegranate molasses imparts the tang and explosive citrusy flavor of fresh pomegranate seeds but is far more convenient and available year-round at Middle Eastern or ethnic grocers. A simple combination of good olive oil, pomegranate molasses, and salt and pepper does wonders for any fish fillet. The lemon/maple syrup combo, added right at the end, smooths out the supertart flavor of the pomegranate. Riesling is a lovely accompaniment.

Four 4-ounce wild salmon fillets
1 tablespoon extra virgin olive oil
1 tablespoon pomegranate molasses
Pinch of kosher salt
Freshly ground black pepper

Zest and juice of 1 lemon,
    preferably Meyer
1 tablespoon maple syrup
1 tablespoon chopped fresh chives

Preheat the oven to 500°F. Rinse and thoroughly dry the fish, then place on an oiled broiling pan. Spoon the oil equally over the fillets, then do the same with the pomegranate molasses. Dust liberally with salt and pepper, place the fish in the oven, and roast for about 10 minutes, until the top is nicely browned and crispy and the inside is barely done.

Meanwhile, put the lemon juice into a small cup, add the maple syrup, and mix. Spoon over the cooked fish, sprinkle on the chives and zest, and serve hot.

Chipotle Calamari with Pink Lentil Crust

Serves 2 as a main course, 4 as a starter

Squid is cheap, full of great protein, and, when prepared properly, delectable. Try this version, which receives a crispy crust from the ground pink lentils and a smoky goodness from the chipotle powder. If you can't find chipotle powder, use any kind of chile powder, provided it's fresh. Try it with a small chilled flask of dry, grassy sake like a daiginjo.

½ pound very fresh calamari steaks

1 large egg yolk

1 dried chipotle chile, whirred in a
    spice grinder (about 1 teaspoon),
    or 1 teaspoon chipotle or other
    chile powder

Freshly ground black pepper

Kosher salt

2 tablespoons dried pink lentils,
    pulverized in a spice grinder

1 tablespoon unsalted butter

1 tablespoon extra virgin olive oil

1 tablespoon sherry vinegar
    or other vinegar

1 tablespoon fresh orange juice

Rinse and dry the squid, then spoon the egg yolk evenly onto one side. Sprinkle on the chipotle powder, black pepper and salt to taste, then the lentil powder.

Melt the butter with the olive oil in a heavy skillet over medium-high heat. Carefully add the squid, crust side down, and cook for a few minutes, until they turn crispy and brown. Turn them over and cook lightly, about 30 seconds. Don't overcook—the squid will turn tough and chewy.

Transfer the squid to warm plates. Add the vinegar and orange juice to the hot pan and use a spatula to scrape up any brown bits that might be sticking, swirling the liquid around. When it reduces to about a tablespoon, pour the sauce over the squid.

◈ Spicy Easy Shrimp

Serves 4 (3 large shrimp per person)

Try to avoid peeled and deveined shrimp, because cleaning before freezing causes off-flavors and weird textures. Buy them whole—it's easy to pull off the heads and legs (they come right off) and devein them by making a shallow slit along the vein (along the back of the shrimp) with a sharp paring knife and pulling the vein out. I like the Gulf pinks best, followed by the Gulf whites.

The spice treatment here brings out the shrimp's natural sweetness. Eat them very hot, right out of the pan if possible. They're great as is, but a little extra pomegranate molasses makes the perfect dipping sauce. They go well with an Alsatian white.

12 large shrimp, peeled and deveined,
    tails left on
2 tablespoons pomegranate molasses,
    plus more for serving (optional)
Generous sprinkling of freshly
    ground black pepper
A few shakes of freshly
    ground cinnamon

Pinch of cayenne
2 tablespoons rice flakes, pulverized
    in a spice grinder
1 tablespoon unsalted butter
1 tablespoon extra virgin olive oil
½ cup chopped fresh cilantro
Kosher or other salt

Rinse and dry the shrimp and put them in a bowl. Add the pomegranate molasses and mix gently. Set the shrimp on a cutting board or other flat surface and sprinkle on some pepper, cinnamon, cayenne, and half the rice flakes. Turn them over and season the other side the same way. Melt the butter with the oil in a heavy skillet over medium-high heat and gently set the shrimp in. When they're nicely browned, after about 2 minutes, flip them over and cook the other side for another minute or so, depending on the size of the shrimp, until well browned.

Place the cilantro on a plate and mound the shrimp over it. Liberally sprinkle them with salt and serve hot with additional pomegranate molasses if you like.

Poultry and Meat

The primal pleasure of eating meat is one of life's great joys, and the meat dishes included here—many of which feature humble and inexpensive cuts—offer a springboard of new ideas. The gutsy, bold recipes that follow represent a few of my favorite ways to prepare chicken, duck, turkey, pork, lamb, and beef.

Good news for carnivores: we're now experiencing a kind of renaissance in single-family ranches that raise small quantities of humanely treated animals that feed largely on grass. You can often find this kind of tasty meat at farmers' markets or at some supermarkets, and it's worth seeking out. You'll pay a little more for it, but this kind of meat does have remarkable flavor.

Allow all roasted meats to rest for at least 10 minutes after cooking; resting allows the hot natural juices to redistribute throughout the meat, while slicing meat straight from the oven forces those juices to flow out, resulting in drier, less flavorful meat.

◈ Miso-Orange-Pepper Roasted Chicken

Serves 4 to 6

This is everything roasted chicken should be: moist, deeply flavorful meat with crisp, citrus-savory skin. You can get great results without brining the chicken first if you use a quality chicken, but it's the brining that makes it so moist. Allow one to six hours to brine the chicken. Try it with an unwooded Chardonnay from Australia, along with a bowl of roasted potatoes and a salad.

1 cup soy sauce

½ cup brown sugar

One 3½-pound chicken, preferably
    organic and free-range

Olive oil spray

2 oranges

2 tablespoons miso

Freshly ground black pepper

Pour the soy sauce into a pasta pot or a clean bucket big enough to hold the chicken, add the sugar, and swirl around to dissolve. Add 2 cups warm water and swirl around some more to dissolve the sugar. Place the chicken into it and add enough cold water to cover completely. Let it brine, refrigerated, for up to 6 hours.

Preheat the oven to 300°F. Rinse off the bird in cold running water and dry it thoroughly with paper towels, including the cavity. Set it, breast side up, on a roasting pan fitted with a rack sprayed with olive oil.

Zest both oranges, place the grated zest in a small bowl, add the miso, and squeeze the juice from one of the oranges into it. Mix together with a fork until you have a creamy miso-orange paste.

Gently separate the skin from the chicken meat (see Note). Spoon the miso paste under the skin, aiming for maximum coverage. Cut the remaining orange into quarters and stuff into the cavity. Spray the skin with olive oil spray, pepper liberally, and roast for 30 minutes. Increase the oven temperature to 375°F, remove the pan from the oven, and flip the chicken over using sturdy tongs so it is now breast side down. Roast for another 30 minutes. Increase the oven temperature to

425°F, remove and flip again, and cook for another 20 minutes to really crisp up the skin.

Remove and let the chicken rest for 15 minutes. Carve and place on a serving platter (I like to separate the white and dark meat on the platter). Squeeze the baked oranges over the meat and sprinkle with salt and pepper to taste.

NOTE: To separate the skin, with the breast side up and using your fingers, very gently begin to pull the skin away from the meat, inch by inch. I sometimes use a small sharp paring knife to slice the muscle that holds the two together, although with enough patience this can be done with just fingers. The idea is to completely separate the skin from the meat so that it's simply lying on top. The miso-orange paste should cover the meat, with the skin acting as a "lid," since the fat will render, mix with the sauce, and continually self-baste the meat.

◈ Crispy Mace Drumsticks

Mace is the wispy, fibrous covering that separates the nutmeg seed from its thick outer husk. It can be challenging to find fresh mace (it's typically sold ground, which means it's already lost most of its flavor), but if you have a reputable local spice store or are willing to order online, this dish can be quite addictive, given its ease of preparation and unique, delicious taste.

I like using drumsticks because of the cooking method: the ample fat of the legs gets exposed to intense heat and produces a lovely spicy crust. Try it with basic fried rice and some winter greens. Good with a lighter Italian or Spanish table red.

1 teaspoon extra virgin olive oil

8 chicken drumsticks, rinsed and dried thoroughly

1 heaping tablespoon freshly ground mace

Liberal sprinkling of kosher salt

1 tablespoon freshly ground black peppercorns

Preheat the oven to 400°F. Rub a tiny amount of olive oil over each drumstick and set them in a baking pan fitted with a rack. (If you spray the rack first with a light coating of olive oil, it prevents sticking; I also like to line the bottom of the pan with foil to facilitate cleanup.) Sprinkle on half the mace, salt to taste, and half the pepper. Flip them over and sprinkle on the other half of the spices. Bake for 40 minutes, flip the legs over, turn up the heat to 425°F, and put them back in for another 15 minutes, or until the skin really browns and crisps up and the meat is ready to fall off the bone.

Minty, Boozy Chicken

Serves 4 to 6

This is like pouring a cooked mojito over stewed chicken, with the rum, lime, and herbs mingling beautifully with the chicken juices. Serve it with rice and a cold, crispy Alsatian white like a Pinot Blanc.

2 tablespoons unsalted butter	1 cup chopped fresh cilantro
2 tablespoons extra virgin olive oil	Zest and juice of 1 orange
1 medium onion, finely minced	Zest and juice of 2 limes, plus 1 lime
5 garlic cloves, roughly chopped	for serving
Pinch of ground cumin	3 tablespoons dark rum
Kosher salt	Olive oil spray
Freshly ground black pepper	1 large onion, sliced into wheels
1 cup chopped fresh mint	8 or so organic chicken pieces

Melt 1 tablespoon of the butter with 1 tablespoon of the oil in a skillet over medium heat. Add the minced onion, garlic, cumin, salt, and pepper, turn the heat down to low, and sauté for about 10 minutes, until the onion softens. Transfer the mixture to a blender, then add the mint and cilantro, zests, juices, and rum and puree. Reserve ½ cup of the puree and use the rest to marinate the chicken for a few hours in the refrigerator.

Preheat the oven to 400°F. Melt the remaining butter with the remaining oil in a large ovenproof skillet over medium heat. Add the chicken pieces, working in batches if necessary, and brown both sides, about 10 minutes.

When nicely browned, transfer the chicken pieces with tongs to a plate. In the same skillet, cook the sliced onion gently for a few minutes, until slightly softened. Return the chicken to the skillet, skin side down, salt and pepper liberally, and pour the marinade over them. Transfer the skillet to the oven and bake for 30 minutes.

Using tongs, flip each piece over, return to the oven, and bake for another 30 minutes, or until the chicken—especially thighs, if you're using them—is fully cooked. Remove the chicken and transfer to a serving platter. Pour the reserved ½ cup puree into the pan and mix it around with a spatula. Pour this sauce over the chicken. Serve with lime wedges and a small bowl of salt to pass around.

Clay-Pot Chicken with Leeks and Lotus Root

Serves 4 or 5

Lotus root has the marvelous property of staying crunchy and toothsome no matter what you do to it. Lotus root is also beautiful, with its whimsically shaped holes, and inexpensive, and it tastes wonderful, like a combination of water chestnuts and parsnips.

When lotus root combines with leeks, which more or less melt as the two cook together, the combination becomes homey and earthy and somehow transcendent; it's the perfect bed for spiced baked chicken.

If you don't own a clay pot, you can use enameled cast iron or a Dutch oven.

1 tablespoon unsalted butter, plus a little for the chicken
1 tablespoon extra virgin olive oil, plus a little for the chicken
2 cups chopped peeled lotus root (about one 10-inch segment)
2 cups chopped leeks, white and light green parts (1 large leek)

Kosher salt
Freshly ground black pepper
½ cup chopped fresh oregano leaves or 2 tablespoons dried
5 skinless boneless chicken thighs, cut into bite-sized pieces
2 tablespoons freshly ground star anise

Preheat the oven to 400°F. Melt the butter with the olive oil in a large skillet or wok over medium heat. Add the lotus root, leek, and salt and pepper to taste. Stir well and sauté for about 10 minutes, until the leek softens. Add the oregano, mix, and transfer the mixture to a clay pot. Spread it out evenly.

In the same large pan or wok, heat a little more butter and olive oil over high heat. Add the chicken, star anise, and some more salt and pepper and cook until the chicken is nicely browned on all sides but still raw in the middle, about 7 minutes. Transfer to the clay pot and bake for 40 minutes. Serve in the clay pot.

◈ Umeboshi Duck Legs

Serves 2

Legs are my favorite part of the duck. They also happen to be the least hassle to cook, at least with this method, which calls for braising them over very low heat and then crisping them in the oven. The piquancy of the umeboshi seems ideally suited for cutting through the considerable amount of fat in duck legs, though most of the fat is rendered and poured off in the first stage of this dish (I refrigerate mine and save it for roasting or sautéing potatoes). I like Champagne with this dish, though a chilled dry rosé works well, too, as does a glass of dry daiginjo sake, preferably from the Niigata region of Japan.

2 meaty duck legs	5 meaty umeboshi, pitted and chopped
Kosher salt	¼ cup umeshu (plum wine)
Freshly ground black pepper	

Remove the visible extra fat from the legs and generously salt and pepper them. Place them, skin side down, in a saucepan or clay pot over low heat, cover, and cook for 45 minutes. Meanwhile, put the umeboshi and plum wine into a blender, puree, and set aside.

After 45 minutes, pour off all the excess fat from the duck, preheat the oven to 450°F, and transfer the legs to a baking pan fitted with a rack. Put some aluminum foil on the bottom to facilitate cleanup. Spoon on some plum sauce and bake for about 30 minutes, or until the legs get deeply brown and crispy.

At this point you can serve the legs as is (they should look really appetizing) and use the extra plum sauce as a dipping sauce. Or you can slice the meat off the bone, gently mix in the remaining plum sauce, and serve it if you prefer your guests not to do any work at all.

Twice-Cooked Lemony Turkey Breast

Makes about 2½ pounds, enough for 8 to 10 hefty sandwiches

I eat turkey all year, not just at Thanksgiving and Christmas. This recipe makes quite a bit; I like having a container full of tasty turkey in the fridge, ready to slake my hunger at any time. It's great in a sandwich, on toasted sourdough bread slathered with chutney, along with a glass of unoaked Chardonnay and a bowl of blue corn tortilla chips.

½ turkey breast, with bone and
    skin (about 3 pounds)
Extra virgin olive oil
1 tablespoon freshly ground coriander
Freshly ground black pepper
Kosher salt

1 tablespoon unsalted butter
½ cup chicken stock or other braising
    liquid
1 teaspoon smoked paprika
Zest and juice of 1 lemon,
    preferably Meyer

Preheat the oven to 425°F. Rinse and dry the turkey and set it on a cutting board. Rub it with a small amount of olive oil and sprinkle on the coriander, pepper, and salt. Melt the butter with 1 tablespoon olive oil in a Dutch oven or other large ovenproof pan with a tight-fitting lid over high heat. Add the turkey breast and cook for about 5 minutes, until it browns a bit. Turn it over and brown the other side.

Add the stock, cover, and place in the oven for 30 minutes. Remove, place the turkey on a cutting board, and let it cool a bit, transferring the pan to the stove. When it's cool enough to handle, slice off all the meat and discard any bones and cartilage (or save them for making stock). Chop the turkey into bite-sized pieces, and put it back in the pot, which should have some juices and tasty brown bits in it.

Turn the heat on the stove back to medium-high and cook until the liquid disappears, up to 15 minutes, stirring often. Add the paprika, stir and cook some more, and then add the lemon zest and juice. Taste again for salt, drizzle with some good-quality olive oil, and serve.

◈ Spicy Star Anise Chicken

Serves 4 or 5

Cooking chicken thighs on aluminum foil in a hot oven renders much of the fat and produces crispy, delicious chicken. Use any freshly ground spice, but I like what star anise does, especially in the liberal quantities I specify here. I cook a large quantity of chicken thighs, because they make fantastic leftovers. Drink a chilled foodcentric white with backbone and good acidity, like an Old World Roussanne, Viognier, or Marsanne.

About 15 boneless chicken thighs, skin on	Plenty of kosher salt
1 tablespoon extra virgin olive oil	6 tablespoons freshly ground star anise
Plenty of freshly crushed black pepper	Olive oil spray
	1 lemon, preferably Meyer, quartered

Preheat the oven to 400°F. Line a baking sheet with foil and lightly spray some olive oil on it. Place the chicken in a bowl, drizzle in a little olive oil, and stir with a spoon, making sure each thigh is coated in oil. Lay the oiled chicken down on the sheet and salt and pepper liberally. Add half the star anise. Flip the thighs over and repeat the coating.

Place the lemon quarters anywhere on the pan and bake for 30 minutes. Using tongs, flip each piece over and continue to roast for 30 minutes, until deeply golden brown and very crispy. Squeeze the baked lemons over the meat and taste for salt—it may need one final dusting.

Spice-Crusted Pork Chops with Plum-Ginger Chutney

Serves 4

Look for the thickest, meatiest pork chops you can find for this dish. Accompany with a baked potato and any of the vegetable sides on pages 181 to 199. The pork pairs well with a light, fruity Grenache or other Old World red.

PORK

2 meaty boneless pork chops, about
    2 inches thick (½ pound each)
Extra virgin olive oil
1 teaspoon freshly ground star anise
1 teaspoon freshly ground coriander
1 teaspoon freshly ground black pepper
1 teaspoon freshly ground green pepper
Kosher salt
1 teaspoon unsalted butter

CHUTNEY

1 tablespoon unsalted butter
¼ cup finely minced shallot
    or red onion
1 tablespoon minced peeled
    fresh ginger
4 plums, peeled, pitted, and chopped
¼ cup umeshu (plum wine)

Preheat the oven to 400°F. Rinse and dry the pork. Drizzle on a little olive oil and rub it all over the meat. Sprinkle on the star anise, coriander, black and green pepper, and salt to taste. Melt the butter with 1 teaspoon olive oil in an ovenproof skillet large enough to hold the pork over medium heat. Swirl around until very hot but not smoking. Add the pork and cook for about 3 minutes, until it begins to form a deeply brown crust (try to let it cook without peeking). Flip it and brown the other side. Place the pan in the hot oven for 10 minutes.

While the pork roasts, make the chutney. Melt the butter in a small skillet over medium heat, add the shallot and ginger, and cook for 2 minutes, until the shallot softens. Add the plums, turn up the heat, add the plum wine, and bring to a rolling boil. Reduce the heat a bit and continue to cook the chutney for about 10 minutes, stirring often, until it reduces to a nice consistency.

Remove the pork and let it rest on a cutting board for 5 minutes, then slice it against the grain into bite-sized pieces. Serve on a warm platter, family style, or on warm individual plates. Top with a heaping tablespoon of chutney per serving.

◈ Clay-Pot Ginger Pork with Figs and Pickled Fennel

Serves 8 generously

Few things are more enticing than the aromas of a big clay pot full of simmering fruity pork. All you need with it is a pot of steamed rice and a bottle of Riesling (well, maybe a vegetable side too). This dish requires very little work to assemble, but it needs about two hours of cooking time. If you don't own a clay pot, you can use enameled cast iron or a Dutch oven.

1 tablespoon unsalted butter
1 tablespoon extra virgin olive oil
1 large onion, minced
1 cup minced peeled fresh ginger
2 pounds pork butt (also called pork shoulder), cut into 1-inch cubes
Liberal dusting of kosher salt
Liberal dusting of freshly ground black pepper

1 cup Ume-Pickled Fennel juice (page 40) or umeshu (plum wine)
10 dried figs (I like Mission), roughly chopped
½ cup carrot juice
Several tablespoons Ume-Pickled Fennel (page 40) for garnish

Preheat the oven to 350°F. Melt the butter with the olive oil in a large clay pot over medium-high heat. Add the onion and ginger and cook until the onion softens, about 5 minutes. Add the pork, salt, and pepper, stir, and cook for another 10 minutes.

Add the pickled fennel juice (or plum wine) and figs, bring to a boil, mix thoroughly, cover, and roast for 1½ hours. Remove from the oven and, using a wooden spoon or a spatula, break apart the pork chunks a bit. Add the carrot juice and return to the oven for another 30 minutes. Taste and adjust the salt. Serve from the clay pot or transfer to warm individual plates and garnish with a mound of pickled fennel.

◈ Minty, Meaty Wontons

These savory, pillowy creations are a snap to prepare, especially if you have an extra pair of hands to help you. Use any kind of ground meat, but the lamb-pork combo is especially good. Serve them with a big salad and a bottle of Rioja.

1 teaspoon unsalted butter	Freshly ground black pepper
¼ cup plus 1 teaspoon extra	¼ pound ground lamb
virgin olive oil	¼ pound ground pork
1 medium onion, diced	12 or so wonton skins
10 scallions, both white and	3 cups loosely packed fresh mint
green parts, minced	leaves, plus a handful for garnish
Pinch of cayenne	1 tablespoon Greek yogurt
Kosher salt	3 tablespoons pine nuts, toasted

Melt the butter with 1 teaspoon of the oil in a wok or large skillet over medium heat. Add the onion, scallions, and cayenne. Salt and pepper generously and sauté for about 5 minutes, until the onion softens. Add the lamb and pork, generously salt and pepper again, and cook, stirring occasionally, until cooked through, about 10 minutes. Pour off any fat that has accumulated and set aside.

Lay the wontons out on a clean cutting board. Spoon some of the meat into a wonton skin and fold to make a triangle (or any other shape you like). Cut off any obviously extra wonton and pinch the ends shut to form a reasonably tight seal. If you lightly dip your fingers in water before pinching, you'll get better results. Repeat with more wonton skins until you've used up all the meat. Place the filled wontons in a bamboo or metal steamer, in several batches if necessary. Bring a pot of water to a boil, place the steamer in the pot over the boiling water, and steam the wontons until soft, about 5 minutes.

Meanwhile, place the mint, ¼ cup olive oil, yogurt, and 2 tablespoons of the pine nuts in a blender and puree. Transfer the wontons to warm individual plates (2 to 3 per person is a good serving size), drizzle the mint sauce over the top, and sprinkle on the remaining pine nuts.

◈ Plummy Braised Beef

Serves at least 6 generously

My never-ending quest for recipes that use less expensive cuts of meat, like chuck roast, and a big pile of beautiful Italian plums gave birth to this combination. Choose slightly underripe plums, whose tartness will make the meat deliciously savory. It's a big, round dish that calls for a light, fruity table wine from Italy or Spain. Have plenty of good crusty bread around and serve with a light green salad.

1 tablespoon extra virgin olive oil	Freshly cracked black pepper
3 pounds boneless chuck roast	1 cup dry red wine
1 tablespoon unsalted butter	½ cup carrot juice
1 medium onion, minced	15 garlic cloves, peeled
Kosher salt	1 cup chopped pitted plums

Heat the olive oil in a heavy skillet with a tight-fitting lid over high heat. Swirl it around until very hot but not smoking. Add the beef and sear on both sides until well browned, about 10 minutes.

Meanwhile, melt the butter in a separate small nonstick pan over medium heat. Add the onion, salt and pepper generously, and sauté until soft, about 5 minutes.

Add the onion to the beef along with the wine, carrot juice, garlic, and plums. Bring to a simmer, cover, lower the heat, and cook until the beef falls apart, about 1½ hours. Don't just disappear, though; keep an eye on it, checking every half hour or so to make sure there is enough liquid in the pan to keep it from burning. If not, add more carrot juice or wine. Serve in a bowl, family style.

◈ Beef "Curry"

Nothing is very traditional or authentic about this curry; hence the quotes. But don't let that stop you from making it—I eat this stuff by the gallon. It's the simmering liquid—a combination of stock, carrot juice, orange juice, and coconut milk—that infuses the fork-tender meat, brightened also by the ginger, with flavor. The preparation requires some active attention: don't let it burn. Thai-style jasmine rice is a natural accompaniment, along with a salad and side of Pickled Ginger (page 38).

1 tablespoon unsalted butter

2 tablespoons extra virgin olive oil

¼ cup minced peeled fresh ginger

4 cloves Garlic Confit (page 41) or
    2 fresh garlic cloves, minced

1 cup minced scallion

1 tablespoon ground coriander

Generous pinch of kosher salt

Freshly ground black pepper

1½ pounds lean beef chuck (also
    sometimes called stewing
    beef), cut into small pieces

1 cup beef stock, preferably
    organic, or hot water

1 cup carrot juice

1 cup coconut milk

1 cup fresh orange juice

Melt the butter with the olive oil in a chef's pan or heavy skillet over medium heat. Add the ginger, garlic, scallion, coriander, salt, and pepper to taste. Stir and sauté for about 5 minutes, until the scallion softens. Add the beef and continue to cook for 5 minutes, until everything is well incorporated. Add the stock, carrot juice, and ½ cup of the coconut milk, bring to a rolling boil, then reduce the heat a little and continue to cook, uncovered, for 30 minutes, which is how long it should take for almost all of the liquid to evaporate.

When it starts to get dry, add the orange juice, raise the heat to medium-high, and cook until it evaporates, 15 minutes or so, being careful not to let it burn. Then add the last ½ cup of coconut milk and cook for another 20 minutes, adding a little water if it threatens to get too dry and burn. Cook until all the liquid disappears and the beef is tender. Taste for salt and serve hot.

◈ Flank Steak with Tamarind-Tomato Chutney

Serves 4 to 6

Flank steak is lean, cooks quickly and easily, and tastes great. Try this simple rendition, panfried with an Indian-inspired spice crust, then thinly sliced and eaten with a chutney made from tamarind syrup, available at any Indian or Middle Eastern market, and tomatoes. A cast-iron pan is a good choice for this dish. You'll need a bottle of old-vine Zinfandel or perhaps Petite Sirah to stand up to its assertive flavors.

CHUTNEY	MEAT
½ cup cored, seeded, and diced tomato	1½ pounds flank steak
1 tablespoon tamarind syrup	1 teaspoon extra virgin olive oil, plus
1 teaspoon maple syrup	a few drops for rubbing the meat
1 teaspoon freshly ground coriander	2 teaspoons freshly ground
Healthy pinch of freshly	black pepper
ground black pepper	1 teaspoon freshly ground coriander
Healthy pinch of kosher salt	1 teaspoon freshly ground star anise
	Kosher salt

Put the tomato, tamarind syrup, maple syrup, coriander, pepper, and salt into a small saucepan and bring to a simmer. Cook over low heat for about 20 minutes, until the mixture is nicely reduced. Turn off the heat and set aside.

Place the flank steak on a cutting board and rub it with a little olive oil. Sprinkle on the pepper, coriander, star anise, and salt to taste. Flip it over and season the other side.

Heat a heavy skillet over high heat, add the oil, and swirl it around to coat. Add the flank steak and cook until the crust is nicely browned, about 3 minutes. Flip it and cook the other side until well browned, another 2 to 3 minutes. This should produce a steak that's rare in the middle and medium toward the edges. Depending on the thickness of the cut, you may want to place the pan in a 400°F oven for

a few minutes, to ensure that it's not too rare in the middle. But even if you have a thicker cut, it shouldn't be in there very long—3 or 4 minutes at most.

Remove when done and let it rest on a cutting board for about 5 minutes (a 10-minute rest is preferable if you can spare the time; a longer resting period usually results in juicier meat). Slice it thinly against the grain and make a nice mound on warmed plates. Spoon some chutney next to it and serve as hot as possible.

◈ Miso Pork

Serves 6

Pork shoulder, also called pork butt, is best when braised at a low temperature for several hours. A Japanese *nabe* (clay pot) is the ideal cooking vessel for this dish, but you can use enameled cast iron or a Dutch oven. Start cooking this dish early on a cold day and serve it with a large bowl of steamed rice, some pickled ginger or fennel (page 38 or 40), and a cup of steaming green tea (or, in my case, probably a glass of Pinot Grigio).

1 tablespoon unsalted butter

2 tablespoons extra virgin olive oil

1 medium onion, minced

1 tablespoon freshly ground star anise

Generous pinch of kosher salt

Generous pinch of freshly
    crushed black pepper

2 pounds boneless pork shoulder,
    trimmed of excess fat, then
    sliced into small chunks

Zest and juice of 2 medium oranges
    (about 1 cup)

½ cup fresh apple juice

2 tablespoons yellow miso

Melt the butter with the olive oil in a clay pot over medium heat. Add the onion, star anise, salt, and pepper. Stir and sauté until the onion is soft, about 10 minutes. Add the pork, stir well, increase the heat to medium-high, and sauté until the pork begins to cook evenly, about 5 minutes. Pour in the orange juice and apple juice and bring to a boil.

Turn the heat to its lowest setting, add the miso, and mix well. Cover and simmer for about 3 hours, checking occasionally to see if the pot needs any liquid (if it does, add some more apple juice). When the pork falls apart, it's ready. Taste for salt and garnish with the zest.

◈ Lavender Lamb Chops

Serves 4

Lamb and lavender create one of those transcendent combinations. Nothing more is needed, except maybe a splash of lemon right at the end to wake it up. Serve with potatoes or rice, along with a vegetable side dish and a glass or two of California Syrah.

1 rack of lamb, about 1½ pounds	1 tablespoon unsalted butter
Liberal dusting of Lavender Salt (page 36)	1 tablespoon extra virgin olive oil
Liberal dusting of freshly ground black pepper	1 lemon, preferably Meyer, zested and quartered

Preheat the oven to 500°F. Rinse and dry the lamb and sprinkle both sides with the salt and pepper. Melt the butter with the olive oil in an ovenproof skillet over high heat until very hot but not smoking. Swirl around, add the lamb, fat side down, and cook for about 5 minutes, until well browned. Flip it and transfer to the oven. Roast for about 5 minutes for medium-rare. Don't overcook the lamb—it's best when still pink in the middle.

Let it rest for 5 or 10 minutes on a cutting board. Slice into individual chops, divide them among the plates, and squeeze some lemon over them, adding a touch more lavender salt and pepper if needed. Top with the zest.

◈ Breakaway Kofta

Ground meat cooks easily and quickly, takes well to spices, is inexpensive, and has all kinds of homey, cozy associations. I call this kofta (Middle Eastern grilled kebabs of ground meat) because of the Middle Eastern–inspired seasonings of pomegranate molasses, coriander, and cinnamon. Try it with a lighter red like Tempranillo or even a Pinot Noir.

1 tablespoon coriander seeds

1 tablespoon star anise

1 teaspoon ground cinnamon

1 tablespoon unsalted butter

1 tablespoon extra virgin olive oil

1 medium red onion, finely
    minced (about 1 cup)

1 tablespoon pomegranate molasses

1 pound ground lamb, beef,
    or a combination

1 large egg

Chiffonade of fresh mint leaves

Preheat the broiler. Toast the coriander seeds and star anise in a small dry skillet over medium heat until fragrant, about 3 minutes. Transfer to a coffee or spice grinder, add the cinnamon, and pulverize to a fine powder.

In the same pan, melt the butter with the olive oil over medium heat, then add the onion and spices and sauté over medium heat until the onion softens, about 3 minutes. Add the pomegranate molasses and continue to sauté for 2 or 3 minutes.

Place the ground meat in a large bowl, add the onion mixture and the egg, and mix well. Form any shape you like, but the classic is the sausage shape. Dust with some more salt and pepper. Place in a broiling pan and broil very close to the heat until well crisped, about 5 minutes. Using tongs, flip them over and broil the other side, another 5 minutes. Transfer to warm plates and top with the mint. Serve hot.

Pasta, Potatoes, and Rice

I often decide what to cook by considering whether I feel like having accompanying rice or potatoes or whether my main course will be pasta. Sometimes the other components will be heavily spiced and bursting with flavor, so all I want is steamed rice or perhaps just a plain baked potato. At other times the potato or rice will play a more starring role, as pasta always does. It's those meals I have in mind for the following recipes.

You can always count on pasta when there's little else in the house, as long as you have some garlic, olive oil, perhaps some canned Italian tomatoes, and a fresh herb or two on hand.

Always cook pasta in plenty of water, and it won't stick together. Use about six quarts or so for a pound of pasta and salt the boiling water with at least a teaspoon before adding the pasta. Cook dried pasta about a minute or two less than recommended on the package, then taste a strand or a piece. If the texture is ever-so-slightly firm, then the pasta is done. Drain it, return it to the pot, add whatever sauce you're using, heat briefly, and taste for salt. Don't oversauce—this is the most common destroyer of what would otherwise be good pasta.

Herby, Creamy Pasta

Serves 2

Ravenous? This hits the hunger meter like nothing else and can be made in about fifteen minutes, start to finish. The addition of Greek yogurt, as opposed to cream, keeps the dish light, yet it tastes creamy and rich. Nice with a big Zinfandel.

1 tablespoon unsalted butter
1 tablespoon extra virgin olive oil
1 large red onion, minced
1 small bunch of scallions, white and
    green parts, minced (about 1 cup)
Lavender Salt (page 36) or kosher salt
Freshly ground black pepper
½ cup loosely packed fresh tarragon
    leaves, plus 1 tablespoon minced

½ cup roughly chopped fresh basil
    leaves, plus 1 tablespoon minced
½ cup carrot juice
2 heaping tablespoons Greek yogurt
½ pound linguine
Freshly grated Parmesan cheese

Bring a large pot of salted water to a boil for the pasta. Meanwhile, melt the butter with the olive oil in a large skillet over medium-low heat, add the red onion, scallion, and salt and pepper to taste. Sauté until soft, about 15 minutes. Transfer to a blender and add the tarragon, basil, carrot juice, and yogurt and blend.

Cook the pasta in the boiling water until al dente, drain, and return to the pot. Gently mix in the sauce and adjust the salt. Transfer to heated bowls and top with the minced herbs and Parmesan.

◈ Crabby, Gingery Linguine

Serves 4

The texture of a softshell crab (a blue crab in its molten state) is a marvel: crunchy, meaty, and soft all at the same time. Fresh softshell crabs are available from May to September in some parts of the country, but frozen ones are just as good in this dish. The ginger and carrot juice keep things bright and refreshing. To wake the dish up even further, add a squeeze of lemon to the pasta at the end. Excellent with a bold, unoaked Chardonnay.

About 2 teaspoons unsalted butter

About 2 teaspoons extra virgin
    olive oil

2 tablespoons minced fresh
    thyme leaves

4 whole softshell crabs

Kosher salt

Freshly ground black pepper

About 3 tablespoons dry white wine

3 tablespoons minced fresh oregano

Pinch of cayenne or other
    red pepper

1 large onion, minced

3 tablespoons minced
    peeled fresh ginger

About 1 tablespoon cream

About 2 tablespoons carrot juice

1 pound linguine

Coarsely grated Asiago cheese

1 lemon, preferably Meyer (optional)

Bring a big pot of salted water to a boil for the pasta.

Meanwhile, melt 1 teaspoon of the butter with 1 teaspoon of the olive oil in a large skillet over medium heat. Add the thyme and crabs, salt and pepper generously, and gently sauté both sides until lightly browned, about 6 minutes. Remove and set aside. Add a splash of wine (about 2 tablespoons) to the pan to deglaze and scrape up any browned bits. Pour that liquid into a blender and wipe out the pan with a paper towel.

Melt a little more butter with a little more olive oil in the same pan over medium heat. Add the oregano, cayenne, onion, and ginger. Salt and pepper liberally and sauté until soft, about 10 minutes. Add the onion mixture to the deglazing liquid in the blender. Add about 1 tablespoon white wine, the cream, and the carrot

juice and puree. Taste for salt. Pour the puree back into the pan and cook for a few minutes to reduce slightly, which will intensify the flavor.

On a cutting board, chop the crab into bite-sized pieces, then divide into 4 equal piles.

Cook the pasta in the boiling water until al dente; try to time it so that it's done just as everything else is done. Drain it and return it to the pot. Add the sauce to the pasta and incorporate it thoroughly, using chopsticks or a wooden spoon. Taste and adjust the salt and pepper. Salty is good for this dish. Work in some cheese to taste.

Divide the pasta among 4 large heated bowls and top with the crab (you may want to briefly reheat the crab in the pan before adding it). Squeeze on the lemon if desired. Top with a little more cheese and serve very hot.

◈ Smoky Red Pasta

Liberal amounts of smoked paprika make this a deeply savory dish that's easy to prepare. The smoked almonds at the end lend a nutty flavor and crunchy texture. Try it with a fruity, lighter red like Grenache or Tempranillo.

1 tablespoon unsalted butter

1 tablespoon extra virgin olive oil

1 medium onion, minced

3 cloves Garlic Confit (page 41), minced, or 1 fresh garlic clove, minced

1 teaspoon smoked paprika

Kosher salt

Freshly ground black pepper

½ cup chopped tomato (canned works well here)

2 heaping tablespoons Greek yogurt

½ cup dry red wine

2 tablespoons minced fresh tarragon

½ pound pasta

2 tablespoons chopped smoked almonds

Bring a large pot of salted water to a boil for the pasta.

Meanwhile, melt the butter with the olive oil in a large skillet or wok over medium heat. Add the onion, garlic, smoked paprika, and salt and pepper to taste and sauté gently until the onion is soft, about 10 minutes.

Transfer to a blender, add the tomato, yogurt, and wine, and puree. Return the puree to the pan and stir in the tarragon. Keep the sauce warm over low heat.

Cook the pasta in the boiling water until al dente, drain, and return to the pan. Add the sauce and mix in gently. Taste for salt. Serve in heated bowls and top with the almonds.

◈ Tomato Orzo

This is a true standby—I almost always have the ingredients lying around, it can be put together in about fifteen minutes, and I never get tired of it. The pomegranate/dried tomato/tarragon combo tastes rich, but it's not; there's not much fat in the dish. The recipe yields a generous amount of sauce, so there may be a few spoonfuls leftover to top poached eggs the next morning. Good with a simple green salad, a crust of chewy sourdough, and a glass of Zinfandel.

10 sun-dried tomatoes

1½ cups orzo

2 cloves Garlic Confit (page 41) or
    1 fresh garlic clove, chopped

3 tablespoons extra virgin olive oil

¼ cup milk

1 teaspoon pomegranate molasses

1 tablespoon apricot or other fruit jam

¼ cup plus 1 tablespoon chopped
    fresh tarragon

Lavender Salt (page 36) or kosher salt

Freshly ground black pepper

Bring a large pot of salted water to a boil for the pasta. When it boils, add the tomatoes and orzo and stir. While that cooks, place the garlic, olive oil, milk, pomegranate molasses, jam, ½ cup tarragon, and salt and pepper to taste in a blender. Set aside.

When the orzo is al dente, drain it. Remove the tomatoes, add them to the blender, and puree with the other ingredients. Return the orzo to the pan and add the sauce in increments: start with about half, mix well, and taste. Keep adding more sauce and mixing until it tastes just right. Adjust the salt and pepper and top with the extra tarragon.

◈ Fennel-Kohlrabi Pasta

Serves 4

This is the essence of winter pasta—deeply filling and satisfying. Fennel is used in both its fresh-bulb form and its dried-seed form; both have their own unique textural and flavor delights that augment the wintery green flavors of the kohlrabi. Have everything prepped before you start cooking. Serve an Old World red, like an Italian Barbera or a Spanish Rioja.

SAUCE

1 tablespoon unsalted butter

1 tablespoon extra virgin olive oil

1 medium red onion, minced

1 leek, white and light green
     parts, trimmed and minced

Kosher salt

Freshly ground black pepper

1 tablespoon freshly ground fennel

½ cup carrot juice

2 tablespoons heavy cream

1 pound linguine

TOPPING

1 tablespoon unsalted butter

1 tablespoon extra virgin olive oil

1 fennel bulb, trimmed and diced

1 medium kohlrabi bulb, diced

Kosher salt

Freshly ground black pepper

1 bunch of kohlrabi leaves, chopped
     (about 1 cup; optional)

Coarsely grated Parmesan cheese for
     garnish

Bring a large pot of salted water to a boil for the pasta.

Meanwhile, melt the butter with the olive oil in a skillet over medium heat. Add the onion, leek, salt and pepper to taste, and fennel and sauté until the onion and leek soften, about 10 minutes. Add the carrot juice and cream, bring to a gentle boil, transfer to a blender, and puree. Return the puree to the pan and keep warm.

Cook the pasta in the boiling water until al dente. Meanwhile, prepare the topping.

In a separate skillet, melt the butter and olive oil over medium heat. Add the fennel and kohlrabi, salt and pepper generously, and sauté for 5 to 7 minutes, until the vegetables soften. Add the kohlrabi leaves if desired and cook for another minute.

When the pasta is cooked, drain it and return to the pot. Mix in the sauce (long chopsticks work well for this task). Add the vegetables, mix, and adjust the salt and pepper. Transfer to hot serving bowls and top with the Parmesan.

◈ Pasta with Peas, Sausage, and Mint

Serves 4

There is a true affinity between mint and peas, and the combination comes even more alive when spread over pasta and topped with sweet-spicy sausage. I prefer frozen baby peas for brightness, flavor, and convenience. Mango sausage is my choice for this recipe, but just about any sausage will work. This goes well with a medium-bodied fruity red like a Spanish Garnacha.

1 tablespoon unsalted butter
1 tablespoon extra virgin olive oil
1 medium onion, diced
3 cloves Garlic Confit (page 41), minced, or 1 fresh garlic clove, minced
4 cups frozen baby peas
Zest and juice of 1 lemon, preferably Meyer

½ cup chicken stock
1 cup chopped fresh mint
1 pound linguine (or other pasta)
1 cup chopped fresh sausage (about ½ pound)
½ cup freshly grated Parmesan cheese

Bring a large pot of salted water to a boil for the pasta.

Meanwhile, melt the butter with the olive oil in a chef's pan or wok over medium heat. Add the onion and garlic and sauté, shaking the pan occasionally, until softened, 3 or 4 minutes.

Add 3 cups of peas to the onion-garlic mixture, stir, and add the lemon juice. Continue to cook for 10 minutes, until the peas are thoroughly warmed.

Add the chicken stock and bring to a boil. Turn off the heat, transfer the mixture to a blender (in batches, if needed), and pulse until coarsely pureed. Add the mint and puree. Return the puree to the pan and keep warm over low heat.

Cook the pasta in the boiling water until al dente. While the pasta cooks, sauté the sausage in a separate small pan until crisped at the edges and cooked through, about 5 minutes. Drain the cooked pasta and transfer to a large serving bowl. Thoroughly mix in the sauce. Taste for salt and top with the sausage and cheese.

◈ Breakaway Fries

Makes three 1-cup servings

I love French fries as much as the next person, especially Belgian-style twice-fried ones. I used to pull out the deep fryer with some regularity, but the process of disposing of huge quantities of leftover oil depressed me—it was hard to throw away, it was wasteful, and using that much oil can't be good for us. I tried making oven-baked fries, but they just didn't do it for me. And then I thought: just slice them thinner and cook them in the trusty chef's pan, using a minimal amount of fat, all of which would be absorbed by the potatoes. Voilà! And to spice them up a bit, I use quite a bit of chipotle powder and top them off with smoked paprika salt. Addictive, these are.

3 cups thinly sliced (shoestring
    cut) Russet potatoes
1 tablespoon unsalted butter
1 tablespoon extra virgin olive oil

1 teaspoon chipotle powder
Smoked Paprika Salt (page 37)
    or kosher salt

Place the cut potatoes in a bowl of cold water and swish them around to get rid of some of the starch. Dry them thoroughly (*really* thoroughly—otherwise they'll splatter in the oil and make a mess) with a clean towel.

Melt the butter with the olive oil in a chef's pan over maximum heat. When it is very hot but not smoking, add the potatoes and sprinkle on the chipotle powder. Shake the pan around vigorously; be sure all the fries are coated with oil and chile powder. Continue to cook over high heat, shaking the pan often (or using a spatula to stir them if you prefer), until they turn golden brown, 5 to 7 minutes. Transfer to a bowl, salt liberally, and eat as quickly as possible.

◈ Pomegranate Potatoes

Easy to make, so quick, and so tasty. One of many reasons to stock up on pomegranate molasses. Serve them hot with a burger or barbecued meat.

4 medium red potatoes, sliced into
    rounds slightly thicker than ¼ inch
Extra virgin olive oil in a spray bottle
1 tablespoon pomegranate molasses

A few shakes of ground cinnamon
Coarse sea salt
Freshly crushed black pepper

Preheat the oven to 500°F. Lay the potato rounds on a wire rack over a baking sheet that's been lined with foil (to facilitate easy cleanup) and spray the potatoes liberally with olive oil. Spoon a small amount of the pomegranate molasses over each round, smearing it around with the spoon, and top with cinnamon, salt, and pepper. Bake until the potatoes start to brown, about 10 minutes. Remove from the oven, flip each one with tongs or chopsticks, repeat the seasoning, and bake for another 5 minutes or so, until nicely browned on both sides.

Mashed Potatoes with Savory Miso Gravy

Serves 4 or 5

Mashed potatoes are the perfect vehicle for this hearty, savory gravy. If you can't find white and red miso, substitute regular yellow miso. I like the potatoes cooked with the skins on, but they can be peeled first for a more refined version.

2 pounds Yukon Gold potatoes	1 tablespoon red miso
½ cup chicken stock	2 tablespoons unsalted butter
¼ cup milk	½ cup finely minced shallot
1 tablespoon white miso	Kosher salt

Bring a large pot of water to a boil. Add the potatoes and cook until tender, about 30 minutes.

Meanwhile, heat the stock and milk together in a small saucepan, add the misos, and stir until dissolved.

Melt the butter in a small saucepan over medium-low heat, add the shallot, and sauté until soft, about 5 minutes. Drain the potatoes and transfer to a mixing bowl. Add the shallot and miso broth, mash well, and add salt to taste.

◈ Orange-Fennel Risotto

Wine, oranges, and Grand Marnier as risotto broth? Yes! The flavors somehow belong together. The diced fennel lends an earthy lightness to an already-light dish.

1 tablespoon unsalted butter	2 cups Arborio rice
1 tablespoon extra virgin olive oil	2 cups dry white wine
½ cup minced shallot	2 cups chicken stock
1 medium fennel bulb, trimmed and diced (about 1 cup), plus 2 tablespoons chopped fronds	Zest and juice (about 1 cup) of 2 oranges
2 tablespoons fennel seeds, ground	Coarse sea salt
Freshly ground black pepper	About 2 tablespoons Grand Marnier

Melt the butter with the olive oil in a saucepan over medium heat. Add the shallot, fennel bulb, ground fennel, and pepper to taste and sauté until the shallot and fennel bulb soften, about 5 minutes. Add the rice and continue to cook for 5 minutes, until the flavors are thoroughly incorporated.

Add 1 cup of the wine, 1 cup of the stock, and all the orange juice. Cook for another 10 minutes, stirring constantly, until most of the liquid disappears, then add the other cup of wine, stir, bring to a boil, and cover. Cook for 10 more minutes, then add the final cup of stock. When it looks done, add plenty of salt and perhaps more pepper (taste it). Pour in a healthy splash of Grand Marnier and mix. Transfer to a large serving bowl, top with the orange zest and fennel fronds, and serve hot.

Habanero Fried Rice

Serves 4 or 5

This dish is spicy-hot, but it's not all about heat: the flavor of the habanero is almost tropical, with notes of passionfruit and other tropical fruits. And the addition of mango does make this dish tropical, though you can substitute just about any fruit such as melon, Asian pear, or kiwi. So satisfying; I come back to this dish again and again, especially when I have some leftover rice from the night before.

1 tablespoon unsalted butter

1 tablespoon extra virgin olive oil

1 medium onion, minced

3 cloves Garlic Confit (page 41), minced, or 2 fresh garlic cloves, minced

1 habanero chile, seeds and veins removed, then minced

Kosher salt

4 to 5 cups cold cooked rice

2 large eggs

Grated zest and juice of 1 lime

1 mango, peeled, pitted, and diced

2 tablespoons minced fresh cilantro

Melt the butter with the olive oil in a chef's pan or wok over medium heat. Add the onion, garlic, and habanero, salt generously, and cook, stirring often, until everything softens, about 5 minutes. Add the rice, mix in thoroughly with a spatula, and cook for another 10 minutes or so, until a uniform mixture results.

Put the eggs and lime juice into a small bowl, beat lightly with a fork, add it to the rice, and stir. Add the mango, mix, taste for salt, and serve in warmed bowls. Top with the lime zest and cilantro.

◈ Citrus Rice Porridge with Umeboshi

Serves 4 to 6

Ask a Japanese person to name a favorite comfort food, and you'll likely hear "okayu," a glutinous rice porridge that comes in as many versions as there are cooks to dream them up. Many Japanese eat it when they catch a cold; okayu is considered the rough equivalent of chicken soup in its restorative power. It's often made with leftover cooked rice, but I prefer using *mochigome* (sticky rice, available at any Asian market) for the porridge—it's chewier, a characteristic of good porridge. It's a good match with an Australian Riesling, served with broiled salmon and a seasonal green salad. It's also great for breakfast (you can replace the wine with chicken stock), with a hot cup of *genmai* cha (green tea with grains of toasted brown rice in it).

2 cups *mochigome* (sticky rice)	Zest and juice of 1 lemon
1 cup carrot juice	1 tablespoon extra virgin olive oil
3 or 4 bay leaves	1 tablespoon maple syrup
10 medium umeboshi, pitted and chopped	Liberal amount of sea salt
	Coarsely ground black pepper
Grated zest and juice of 2 oranges	½ cup dry white wine

Rinse the rice well and put into a saucepan with 3 cups water, the carrot juice, and the bay leaves. Cover and bring to a boil.

Meanwhile, put the umeboshi, citrus juices and zest, olive oil, maple syrup, and salt and pepper to taste in a blender and puree.

When the rice boils, turn the heat down to low and cook for about 10 minutes. Pour in the citrus liquid and stir for a few minutes. Add the wine, stir, and cook until the rice is soft and chewy, about 5 minutes. Depending on the consistency of porridge you desire, you can either stop now or add more water. Taste for salt. Serve very hot in warmed bowls.

◈ Grilled Rice Triangles

It's hard to imagine a better way to end a meal than with *yakinigiri*—grilled rice triangles with a bit of filling. These are so common in Japan that even convenience stores offer an impressive selection of them.

The very nature of yakinigiri leaves them wide open to interpretation (typically, in my case, to whatever's lying around in the fridge), which is a boon to breakaway cooks. For this version I use chopped umeboshi, slightly sweetened with maple syrup, but you can use leftover pork, beef, chicken, salmon, leftover grilled vegetables, or even ripe fruit. Children love them (I think it's the shape). It's a good way to use up leftover cooked rice. Use half a cup of rice per yakinigiri.

3 meaty umeboshi, pitted and finely chopped	4 cups cooked white rice
	2 tablespoons soy sauce
1 tablespoon maple syrup	1 tablespoon unsalted butter, melted

Mix the chopped umeboshi with the maple syrup in a small cup and set aside.

Using your hands, form a loose ball with a packed ½ cup of the rice. Then make a small well in the middle (by simply pressing down with your fingers) and spoon in about a teaspoon of the umeboshi mixture. Close it up and make a ball again, but this time do it tighter—use some force and really pack it in. Then shape it into a triangle. Make 7 more the same way.

Place the soy sauce and butter in a small bowl and stir with a fork. Heat a dry nonstick skillet over medium heat, brush some soy-butter on the surface of 4 yakinigiri, and place them in the hot pan. Cook for a few minutes, until crispy and brown, flip them over, brush on a little more soy-butter, and cook the other side. Repeat with the next round and serve hot or at room temperature.

◈ Shiitake Genmai Lemon Risotto

Serves 5

This baked rice dish made with *genmai* (short-grain brown rice) is nothing like a traditional Italian risotto, but we have firmly established by now that we're not as interested in purity of tradition as we are in good flavors. The result is earthy, dense, and rib-sticking. It can be the star of a meal, though it's good along with a piece of broiled fish and steamed vegetables.

1 quart chicken broth, preferably organic
2 tablespoons unsalted butter
1 tablespoon extra virgin olive oil
1 large onion, minced
Freshly ground black pepper

3 large dried shiitake mushrooms, pulverized in a spice grinder (about 1 cup)
2 cups short-grain brown rice
2 tablespoons soy sauce
Zest and juice of 1 lemon

Preheat the oven to 375°F. Bring the broth and 1½ cups hot water to a simmer in a small saucepan.

Meanwhile, melt the butter with the olive oil in a clay pot or an ovenproof dish with a tight-fitting lid over medium heat. Add the onion and pepper to taste and cook until tender, about 5 minutes. Add the powdered shiitake, mix well, and cook for a few more minutes. Add the rice, stir, and cook for a few more minutes, until the rice is thoroughly incorporated. Pour in the simmering broth and add the soy sauce and lemon juice. Bring to a rolling boil, stir well, cover, and transfer to the oven. Bake for 80 minutes. Don't peek! Remove and garnish with the grated lemon zest before serving.

Vegetable Sides

In some ways this chapter is the heart of breakaway cooking. The idea is to take humble, nonexotic vegetables—ones we see every day, like carrots, cauliflower, beets, peas, broccoli—and do something unique and interesting with them. As I've stressed throughout this book, your vegetables will taste better if you buy them from local farmers who use organic methods, but the dishes are still good with supermarket veggies.

Butternut Squash "Pizzettas"

Makes 14 to 16

The greatest thing about these things, aside from their scrumptiousness and ease of preparation, is their versatility. Just as with pizza, you can come up with any "topping" you like or have on hand. In this version I use a basil puree topped with pistachios, but all herbs work; tarragon is especially nice with goat cheese. Try a Japanese version with soy sauce and minced ginger, or make some spiced with ground star anise and fennel seed. These disappear instantly when served at parties.

1 medium butternut squash
½ cup extra virgin olive oil,
    plus oil for brushing
Kosher or other salt

Freshly ground black pepper
2 cups fresh basil leaves
1 garlic clove, chopped
¼ cup chopped pistachios

Preheat the oven to 400°F. Peel and slice the squash into wheels as described in the Note on page 64. Place on an oiled baking sheet, brush on some olive oil, and sprinkle with salt and pepper to taste. Bake for about 30 minutes, until almost done.

Meanwhile, put the basil, garlic, and olive oil into a blender and puree. When the squash starts to brown and looks almost ready to eat, spoon on some of the sauce, sprinkle with pistachios, and bake for another 5 minutes. Serve very hot. I like to slice them, pizza style, into 6 bites per pizzetta.

Creamy, Spicy Carrots

Serves 4

Cardamom and saffron give this dish a distinctly Indian character, but it fits right in as a side dish at any breakaway meal. One of my favorite ways to prepare carrots.

1 tablespoon unsalted butter
4 cups shredded carrot (3 medium-large carrots)
Kosher salt
Freshly ground black pepper
10 cardamom seeds, pods removed, then crushed with a mortar and pestle or in a coffee or spice grinder

Small pinch of saffron threads, minced
1 cup milk
¼ cup finely chopped pistachios

Heat the butter in a saucepan, large skillet, or wok over maximum heat. Add the shredded carrot, salt and pepper generously, stir, and add the cardamom and saffron. Cook for a few minutes to incorporate the flavors, shaking the pan constantly. Add the milk and bring to a boil (it will boil quickly), then cook over low heat until the liquid disappears, about 20 minutes. Taste for salt and sprinkle on the chopped pistachios.

◈ Cauliflower "Couscous" with Basil-Lemon Sauce

Serves 8

For the longest time, I fought cauliflower. I usually prepared it Indian style, heavily spiced and cooked whole, but shied away from the floret stir-fry or other recipes with whole florets. Here the cauliflower is finely chopped so it resembles couscous and will absorb other flavors. Try this excellent version, but also try replacing the sauce with different combos, like tamarind or pomegranate dressing for a sweet/tart rendition, or add some chipotle for a hot and smoky version. Great with a glass of unoaked Chardonnay.

1 tablespoon unsalted butter

1 tablespoon extra virgin olive oil

1 medium red onion, finely diced

1 medium head of cauliflower, stalks and stems discarded, florets finely diced

Kosher salt

Freshly ground black pepper

¼ cup Basil-Lemon Sauce (page 47)

2 tablespoons fresh basil chiffonade

Melt the butter with the olive oil in a chef's pan or wok large enough to hold all the cauliflower over high heat. Add the onion and sauté until the onion softens, about 2 minutes. Add the cauliflower, stir thoroughly, salt and pepper liberally, and cook until the cauliflower softens, about 10 minutes. Add 2 tablespoons of the sauce and cook until tender and fragrant, another 10 minutes. Adjust the salt, add the remaining 2 tablespoons sauce, mix thoroughly, and transfer to a serving bowl. Top with the basil chiffonade.

Beet "Tartare"

Finely diced cooked beets livened up with tangerines, olive oil, vinegar, and Greek yogurt are a great accompaniment to any roasted meat or fish, but I sometimes eat a big bowl for lunch. Try some with lightly dressed arugula or other lettuce: just form a ring on the plate with the greens and arrange the beets in the center. Serve them with a glass of chilled dry Sauvignon Blanc.

8 medium beets (I like a combination of red, golden, and Chiogga)
Zest and juice of 1 large tangerine
2 tablespoons extra virgin olive oil
1 tablespoon champagne vinegar
2 tablespoons Greek yogurt
Maccha Salt (page 36) or kosher salt
Freshly ground black pepper

Bring a large pot of water to a boil. Add the beets, cover, and simmer for about 40 minutes, or until the tip of a knife slides in without much resistance. Drain and run cold water over them. Squeeze them very lightly and slip off the skins; they should come right off.

Working with one at a time, finely mince all the beets (this will take a little time—be patient; it's worth it) and transfer to a serving bowl. If you're using different kinds of beets, keep them in separate bowls, since mixing them will run the colors together.

Add the tangerine zest and juice, olive oil, and vinegar and mix well. Gently mix in the yogurt and serve. I like to scoop some into a ½-cup measuring cup and carefully shake it out onto a plate, forming a little beet hockey puck, then repeat with the different-colored beets. Sprinkle with salt and pepper to taste.

◈ Red Chard, Avocado, and Blood Orange with Mango-Chutney Dressing

Serves 4

This side dish has it all: creamy avocado, tart orange, savory greens, zesty chutney, and crunchy toasted almonds. Serve as a salad or a side dish alongside a piece of grilled fish.

3 bunches of red chard, stems
    and spines discarded
Kosher or other salt
Freshly black ground pepper
1 large ripe avocado, peeled, pitted,
    and cut into bite-sized pieces
1 large blood orange, zested and
    sectioned

2 tablespoons extra virgin olive oil
1 tablespoon brown rice
    or other vinegar
2 tablespoons mango or other
    store-bought chutney
Handful of slivered almonds, toasted

Steam or boil the chard leaves for 3 to 4 minutes, then plunge them into cold water. Gently squeeze as much moisture as possible from the chard. You should end up with a ball a little bigger than a baseball. Chop the chard on a cutting board, salt and pepper liberally, and divide into 4 equal portions. Make a small chard wreath on each of 4 plates and fill the middle with avocado pieces and orange sections, artfully arranged however you like.

Put the olive oil, vinegar, chutney, and salt and pepper to taste into a jar and shake vigorously. Carefully drizzle everything with the dressing, using a light hand, then scatter the almonds and grated orange zest over them. Give each plate a final flick of salt and pepper.

◈ Fenneled Greens and Oranges

Serves 5 or 6

The crunch of raw fennel combined with the toothy goodness of cooked greens and the brightness of orange zest and juice results in a beautiful accompaniment to roast chicken or barbecued meat. In this recipe I use collard greens, but the dish can be made with chard, mustard greens, kale, Asian greens, spinach, or any other dark leafy green you can think of. Lavender salt adds a nice floral touch, but you don't need it: sel gris, kosher, or any other salt is fine. A grassy, stony Sauvignon Blanc from New Zealand is excellent with it.

3 large bunches of collard greens
or other winter greens,
tough spines discarded
1 medium fennel bulb, trimmed,
cored, and sliced as thinly as
possible across the grain
3 tablespoons extra virgin olive oil

1 tablespoon brown rice
or other vinegar
Zest and juice of 1 small orange
1 teaspoon fennel seeds, finely ground
Lavender Salt (page 36) or kosher salt
Freshly crushed black pepper

Bring a large pot of salted water to a rolling boil, add the greens, and cook briefly, about 4 minutes, until they are tender. Drain, rinse with cold water, and, using your hands, squeeze out as much water as possible so the greens will act like a sponge.

Transfer the greens to a cutting board and chop them roughly. Place in a serving bowl and add the sliced fennel.

Shake the oil, vinegar, and orange juice together in a jar. Add the dressing to the greens and mix. Sprinkle in the ground fennel and salt and pepper to taste. Adjust the seasonings to taste and top with the orange zest.

Gingered Green Beans

Serves 4

I eat a lot of green beans, sometimes as an accompaniment to a main dish, but just as often as a quick, tasty lunch. Sautéing them over high heat with the pickled ginger gives the beans a nice pungency and crunchy texture.

1 tablespoon unsalted butter

1 tablespoon fruity extra virgin olive oil

1 pound green beans, trimmed

Generous pinch of freshly
    ground black pepper

½ cup Pickled Ginger (page 38),
    julienned

1 tablespoon soy sauce

2 tablespoons fresh orange juice

Melt the butter with the olive oil in a chef's pan or wok over maximum heat, add the beans and pepper, and cook, shaking the pan or stirring often, until they start to brown, about 5 minutes. Add the ginger, soy sauce, and orange juice, stir, turn the heat down to medium-low, and cover. Continue to cook, covered, for 7 minutes or so, until the beans are soft. Remove the lid and cook until the liquid disappears. Transfer to a warm serving bowl to pass around.

◈ Golden Beets Roasted in Lavender Salt

Serves 4

Nothing could be simpler than rubbing some olive oil and salt into beets, wrapping them up in foil, and roasting them in the oven. There is something almost alchemistic about the marriage of the floral lavender and the sweet-earth beet. Think of these as your starch—try them instead of the usual baked potatoes or as a side dish with any main course.

4 large golden beets
Extra virgin olive oil

Freshly ground black pepper
Lavender Salt (page 36)

Preheat the oven to 400°F. Cut four 12-inch square sheets of aluminum foil. Rub the beets with some olive oil and place each one on a sheet of foil. Generously sprinkle on some pepper and even more generously sprinkle on some lavender salt (you'll need about a tablespoon of salt per beet). Wrap them up tightly in the foil, place in the oven, and bake for 1 hour.

Test for doneness by piercing with a sharp knife—it should go through with very little resistance. Remove from the oven, take off the foil, and let them cool a bit. When cool enough to handle, slip off the skins, which will be the saltiest part. Roughly chop up the beets, drizzle on a little olive oil, and serve.

◈ Baby Artichokes Braised in Yuzu

Serves 4

Baby artichokes are not immature: they're small because they grow near the bottom of the plant, usually in the shade. They lack much of the thistly fiber of their larger brethren and, with a simple preparation, can be eaten, with a great deal of pleasure, whole. The yuzu used here is well worth seeking out (see page 33), but this method works well with any kind of braising liquid. Try braising with a light herb vinaigrette or just some chicken stock.

3 tablespoons white vinegar

15 baby artichokes

1 teaspoon unsalted butter

1 teaspoon fruity extra virgin olive oil

Tangerine Salt (page 36) or kosher salt

Freshly ground black pepper

¼ cup dry white wine

1 tablespoon yuzu juice or mixed fresh lemon and lime juice

1 tablespoon maple syrup

Fill a bowl large enough to hold the artichokes with cold water and the vinegar. One by one, cut off the stems of the chokes and pull off the tough outer leaves (about 5 layers) so that they resemble tight rosebuds. Cut off the green tip of each choke (about a quarter of the entire thing) and discard. Cut them in half vertically and toss them into the acidulated water to keep the artichokes from discoloring. When you're finished trimming and are ready to cook, dry them with a clean towel.

Melt the butter with the olive oil in a chef's pan or wok over high heat and add the artichokes. Salt and pepper them generously and cook, shaking the pan often, until brown spots begin to appear, after about 5 minutes. Meanwhile, combine the wine, yuzu juice, and maple syrup in a cup and swirl it around. Have a lid handy, add the liquid to the pan, and cover immediately. Turn down the heat to very low and cook for about 10 minutes. Serve hot.

Baked Peas with Tarragon, Yogurt, and Pistachios

Serves 4 or 5 generously

Frozen peas are a gift to the breakaway cook: their creamy, earthy goodness bursts with flavor, and they couldn't be easier to store and prepare. The pesto-like tarragon emulsion, made even creamier by the addition of Greek yogurt, really brings out the best in them, and the sprinkling of pistachios on top lends a lovely toasted, nutty texture. Try them with a broiled fish fillet and a glass of grassy Sauvignon Blanc.

1 pound frozen baby peas
½ cup loosely packed fresh
    tarragon leaves
2 scallions, white and green
    parts, chopped

2 tablespoons extra virgin olive oil
¼ cup Greek yogurt
½ cup chopped pistachios

Preheat the oven to 500°F. Put the peas in a clay pot or a small Dutch oven and gently heat them on the stove until they thaw, stirring occasionally.

Meanwhile, put the tarragon, scallions, olive oil, yogurt, and ¼ cup of the pistachios into a blender and puree. Gently mix into the peas, sprinkle the top with extra chopped pistachios, and bake for about 15 minutes—about the time the top will begin to brown. Remove and serve in your best serving bowl.

◈ Maccha Pearl Onions

Frozen pearl onions are every bit as good as fresh, which are a nuisance to peel. The green tea in the maccha salt brings out their sweetness and gives them an alluring, almost ethereal shade of light green. They're a lively and visually striking accompaniment to any main dish.

1 tablespoon unsalted butter
10 ounces frozen pearl onions
1 tablespoon brown rice or other
    vinegar

Maccha Salt (page 36)
Freshly ground black pepper

Melt the butter in a medium skillet over medium heat. Add the frozen onions and cook until thoroughly warmed, about 10 minutes. Add the vinegar, stir, and turn up the heat a bit. When they're very hot, add several generous pinches of maccha salt and some pepper. Serve hot.

Broccoli "Rice"

Serves 4

Finely minced broccoli resembles rice more than it does a vegetable, so I serve this in lieu of a starch alongside a piece of grilled meat or fish. It's rare that a guest doesn't ask for seconds, so consider doubling the recipe. A fresh, fruity Viognier makes it shine even more.

1 tablespoon unsalted butter

1 tablespoon extra virgin olive oil

1 large onion, minced

Kosher salt

Freshly ground black pepper

1 medium head of broccoli, minced to the consistency of rice grains

DRESSING

2 tablespoons Greek yogurt or plain yogurt

1 tablespoon yuzu juice or other citrus juice

5 large shiso leaves, chopped, or 2 tablespoons chopped fresh mint

Melt the butter with the oil in a chef's pan or wok over medium-low heat. Add the onion and salt and pepper liberally. Cook, stirring occasionally, until softened, about 7 minutes.

Add the broccoli. Continue to cook for 10 minutes, until the broccoli is cooked through.

Meanwhile, whisk together the dressing ingredients. Add the dressing to the cooked broccoli, mix well, cook for another few minutes to incorporate the flavors, and serve very hot.

Sweets

For fifteen years, the period I lived in Japan, I rarely ate dessert, because they were rarely available. Since I moved back to San Francisco, the allure of a final bite of something sweet has beckoned once again. What follows are some very simple dishes that can be made with little time, effort, or expertise, yet their flavor combinations will, I hope, surprise and delight you.

◈ Maccha Truffles

These little gems take only a few minutes of prep time, some cooling time in the fridge, then a few more minutes to shape the chocolate into balls. Wrapped up in a pretty box, they make beautiful gifts for friends.

1 cup heavy cream

¼ cup maple syrup

2 tablespoons brown sugar

2 tablespoons maccha

12 ounces bittersweet chocolate, finely chopped

Pinch of Maccha Salt (page 36) or kosher salt

Bring the cream to a simmer in a small saucepan over gentle heat, add the maple syrup and brown sugar, and stir until dissolved, about 2 minutes. Add 1 tablespoon of the maccha, stir until dissolved, and set aside.

Place the chocolate in a large mixing bowl and pour in the cream mixture. Mix thoroughly and pour onto a baking sheet lined with parchment paper. Smooth it out with a rubber spatula. Cool in the refrigerator for about an hour.

Scoop out a heaping teaspoonful and make a ball using your palms. Repeat until all the chocolate is used—you should end up with about 50 truffles. Line them up on a tray or plate and dust them with the remaining tablespoon of maccha, using a fine sieve. Top with a very light sprinkling of maccha salt.

◈ Persimmons Grand Marnier

An elegant, three-minute dessert. This works equally well with bananas.

1 tablespoon unsalted butter
Dash of ground cinnamon
2 Fuyu persimmons, peeled and
sliced into irregular shapes

About 2 tablespoons Grand Marnier,
plus more for serving (optional)

Melt the butter in a small saucepan over medium-high heat, add the cinnamon and persimmon pieces, and sauté for a few minutes. Add the liqueur, being careful of the dramatic high flame that will result. Transfer to a warm plate and serve. Add an extra splash of Grand Marnier if you like.

Soft Chocolate Maccha Cakes

The bitter maccha provides a nice foil for the overall richness of the cakes, and its dreamy green color plays against (and with) the chocolate. These cakes are caloric, but surely we are all allowed an occasional ambrosial fat bomb. They can be served about fifteen minutes after beginning the prep, making them dangerously easy and guaranteed to please a crowd.

2 large eggs plus 2 yolks

¼ cup brown sugar

8 tablespoons (1 stick) unsalted butter, plus a little for the ramekins

4 ounces bittersweet chocolate

1 tablespoon flour, plus a little for dusting the ramekins

½ teaspoon maccha

Preheat the oven to 425°F. Whisk the eggs, yolks, and brown sugar together in a medium bowl. Set aside.

Place the butter and chocolate in a microwave-safe bowl and heat in the microwave on medium power for about 2 minutes, until the chocolate is mostly melted. Meanwhile, lightly butter and then lightly flour four 4-ounce ramekins or other molds and tap out any excess flour.

Whisk together the melted chocolate/butter mixture and then add the egg mixture. Quickly whisk in the 1 tablespoon flour until combined. Use just a few strokes; it will stay silkier if you don't overbeat it. Pour this batter evenly into the ramekins.

Place the ramekins in the oven and bake for 6 to 7 minutes. Use a timer, because it's easy to overbake these. The sides should be firm, but the middle should be very soft. Remove and invert each ramekin onto a separate serving plate; it should just shake loose. Place the maccha in a small sieve and tap some tea over each plate, as with powdered sugar.

◆ Asian Pear–Ginger Crisp

Serves 6 generously

This is a ginger-laced version of a classic fruit crisp. It's a homey and delicious concoction, perfect with vanilla ice cream and an espresso.

FRUIT

4 medium Asian pears, peeled,
 cored, and thinly sliced

Juice of ¼ lemon

1 tablespoon unsalted butter

¼ cup 1-inch matchsticks
 peeled fresh ginger

1 tablespoon maple syrup

CRISP/STREUSEL

½ cup flour

¼ cup oats

¼ cup plus 2 tablespoons
 light brown sugar

Generous pinch of kosher salt

¼ teaspoon ground cinnamon

Generous pinch of ground nutmeg

4 tablespoons (½ stick) very cold
 unsalted butter

Preheat the oven to 375°F. Put the pears in a bowl and squeeze the lemon juice over them. Melt the butter in a small skillet over medium heat and add the ginger. Stir, sauté for a minute or two, until it softens a bit, and add the maple syrup. Continue to cook over medium heat for 3 minutes to blend the flavors thoroughly. Add the ginger to the pears and carefully place the fruit mixture in the bottom of a baking dish or pie pan.

Combine the flour, oats, brown sugar, salt, cinnamon, and nutmeg. Slice the cold butter into the dry ingredients and, using your fingertips, incorporate the butter until the dough starts to crumble. Sprinkle the crisp on top of the fruit and place in the middle of the oven. Bake for about 35 minutes, until it starts to brown on top. Serve hot, at room temperature, or cold.

◈ Jasmine Biscotti with Almonds

Makes about 30 biscotti

I once happened to be making a pot of jasmine tea and became intoxicated with its heady aromas. I decided to bake something savory-sweet with the fine powder I made out of the tea leaves, and biscotti seemed like a good candidate. It was; I now almost always have them around. They'll keep for a few weeks stored in an airtight jar, so you can bake them far in advance of a dinner party. And since the recipe makes so many, you can send your guests home with a few.

8 tablespoons (1 stick) unsalted butter

2½ cups flour

1 teaspoon baking powder

3 tablespoons jasmine tea, finely ground in a spice grinder

1½ teaspoons ground cinnamon

3 large eggs

1 cup organic cane sugar or light brown sugar

1 teaspoon vanilla extract

4 ounces almonds, chopped

Preheat the oven to 375°F. Gently melt the butter (I use the microwave on medium power) and set aside. Combine the flour, baking powder, powdered jasmine tea, and cinnamon in a bowl.

Cream the eggs and sugar until fluffy in a large bowl. Add the melted butter and vanilla and gently mix together. Sprinkle in the flour mixture, add the chopped almonds, and mix until combined.

Place the dough on a floured surface and divide in half. Using your hands, shape each half into a long log, roughly 1 inch thick, 15 inches long, and 3 inches wide. Place the logs next to one another on a cookie sheet and bake for 25 minutes, until the edges begin to brown a bit.

Remove them from the oven and reduce the oven temperature to 275°F. Once the logs have cooled down just enough for you to touch them comfortably (about 5 minutes), cut them on the diagonal into pieces of whatever thickness you like (a little less than an inch seems to work best) and place them back on the cookie sheet, cut side up. Bake for another 20 minutes, remove, and let cool.

◈ Rosemary-Plum Sorbet

Makes a little less than 1 quart

The combination of savory and sweet is a most welcome trend at many restaurants and gelaterias these days. This backyard version (rosemary grows easily just about everywhere, and plum trees dominate the landscape here in San Francisco) of quick sorbet is always a treat.

4 medium-large ripe plums, peeled, pitted, and chopped (about 1 cup)

1 heaping tablespoon minced fresh rosemary

2 cups fresh spring water

½ cup organic cane sugar or white sugar

½ cup maple syrup

Put the plums and rosemary into a saucepan with the water, bring to a simmer, and add the sugar and maple syrup. Stir until dissolved, 1 to 2 minutes, and cool in an ice bath.

Pour the plum mixture through a fine sieve and use a rubber spatula to force as much of the pulp as possible into a bowl. Transfer the liquid to a plastic jug or glass bottle and set in the freezer for about 20 minutes or for several hours in the fridge. Pour into an ice cream maker and follow the manufacturer's directions. Transfer to a plastic ice cream container and freeze for at least 2 hours before serving. Keeps for a month.

◈ Star Anise–Lemon Sorbet

Makes slightly less than 1 quart

This lemony, aromatic sorbet never fails to elicit requests for the recipe. The bouquet of the star anise pairs nicely with the lemon and tempers the sweetness of the sorbet. Thoroughly chill the lemon mixture before pouring it into the ice cream maker. Serve it with Jasmine Biscotti (page 208) and a small piece of seasonal fruit.

2 cups spring water

1 cup organic cane sugar or white sugar

½ cup brown sugar

1 tablespoon finely ground star anise

Zest of 1 lemon, preferably Meyer, chopped (about 1 tablespoon)

1½ cups lemon juice (about 6 large Meyers or a few more regular lemons)

Bring the water to a boil in a small saucepan. Add the cane sugar, brown sugar, and star anise and cook for about a minute, until the sugars dissolve. Transfer to a bowl and cool in an ice bath. Pour through a fine sieve and into a 1-quart or larger plastic or glass bottle. Add the lemon zest and juice. Shake and set in the freezer for about 20 minutes to get it nice and cold or for several hours in the fridge.

When it's icy cold, pour into an ice cream maker and follow the manufacturer's directions. Transfer to a plastic tub and freeze for a few hours before serving. Keeps for a month.

Galangal–Brown Sugar Ice Cream

Makes 1 quart

This is an insanely rich and delicious ice cream, but the richness is tempered by the floral pungency of the galangal. You can successfully substitute half-and-half for the heavy cream, if you're trying to limit your calories.

2 cups heavy cream	¾ cup plus ½ cup brown sugar
2 cups whole milk	2 vanilla beans, split with a knife
1 cup roughly chopped peeled galangal	6 large egg yolks

Bring the cream, milk, galangal, and ¾ cup of the sugar to a simmer in a medium-large pot, stirring occasionally. Scrape the seeds out of the vanilla beans and add to the cream mixture.

Meanwhile, whisk the remaining ½ cup sugar with the egg yolks. When the cream mixture is hot, whisk about ½ cup of it into the yolks. Add the tempered yolks to the remaining cream mixture and stir. Pour the hot cream through a fine sieve into a bowl set over an ice bath (to prevent the yolks from overcooking).

Chill the ice cream base thoroughly and process in an ice-cream/gelato maker according to the manufacturer's instructions. Transfer to an ice cream container and freeze for at least 2 hours before serving. Keeps for a month.

Index